HOW CON GAMES WORK

HOW CON GAMES WORK

M. ALLEN HENDERSON

Citadel Press / Secaucus, N.J.

Thanks are due Detective Robert Thiede of the Denver Police Intelligence Division, Craig A. Harrison, M.D., and Dan Eisenberg, president of Tracers Company of America, for contributing information for *Flimflam Man;* to Rose-Marie Strassberg for her painstaking editing; and to Frances Porter, art director, for the special attention she has given this book. I am also indebted to several bunco friends and acquaintances, who shall here remain nameless, for giving me a personal insight into the confidence experience.

For Molly Henderson, with love

Contents

He knew that the true hustler could come back to the same mark and hustle him two, three, four, five, six times and still be regarded as a friend. The hustler who used up a mark in one shot was bogus, an amateur, a waster of his talent. And Gronevelt knew that the true hustler had to have his spark of humanity, his genuine feeling for his fellowman, even his pity of his fellowman. The true genius of a hustler was to love his mark sincerely. The true hustler had to be generous, compassionately helpful and a good friend. This was not a contradiction. All these virtues were essential to the hustler. They built up his almost rocklike credibility. And they were all to be used for the ultimate purpose. When as a true friend he stripped the mark of those treasures which he, the hustler, coveted or needed for his own life. And it wasn't that simple. Sometimes it was for money. Sometimes it was to acquire the other man's power or simply the leverage that the other man's power generated. Of course, a hustler had to be cunning and ruthless, but he was nothing, he was transparent, he was a one-shot winner, unless he had a heart.

Reprinted by permission of the Putnam Publishing Group
From *Fools Die* by Mario Puzo
Copyright © 1978 by Mario Puzo

1.

Everybody Loves an Outlaw

Hain't we got all the fools in town on our side?
And ain't that a big enough majority in any town?
The King, a confidence artist
Mark Twain, *Huckleberry Finn*

The world has been crawling with con artists ever since the good old days in the Garden of Eden, when Eve was suckered into eating an apple by a snake. We all lost big as a result of that scam. Of course, she hadn't been around much; but it is my belief that she would fall for it all over again given a second chance, and provided the snake were to throw in a microwave for good measure.

You can't really blame her. It is human nature to go for a deal that sounds too good to be true, even when one is being propositioned by a snake in the grass. Or, in Eve's case, by a snake in a tree. It is easy to criticize after the fact, but I'll bet you a dollar you'd eat that apple now if it were presented by the right snake in the right way.

After all this time we ought to know better than to fall for the same old tricks, and yet we do fall for them every day of the year, to the tune of millions of dollars. A sucker is not necessarily a fool, and he is not necessarily greedy or larcenous, either. Anyone, from a simple farm boy to an experienced con man, can be a mark, sometimes even when he knows he is being conned. In this chapter we will sketch a general picture of the confidence artist, or con man, and explain something of the chemistry between him and the mark. The premise is that you stand a better chance of coming out ahead when you understand the motivations at work in the confidence game—your own as well as those of the con man.

THE OUTLAW AS HERO

The con artist wouldn't stand a chance if people weren't predisposed to admire and romanticize criminals—not your average criminal, of course, but the intelligent, dashing kind of lawbreaker that always gets away. Every country has its outlaw heroes, sly and slippery devils who manage to elude the authorities and get the last laugh every time. Norse, African, and American Indian mythologies are filled with entertaining stories about trickster gods, and the Greek god Hermes served as patron and protector of thieves when he wasn't busy winging messages around. Men have been immortalized for their illegal acts since the dawn of recorded history, the tales of their exploits handed down from generation to generation.

Chances are that, even if your parents were law-abiding souls who taught you to mind the rules and keep your nose to the grindstone, you were raised on stories of Robin Hood, Billy the Kid, and Zorro. Even the most outspoken advocates of law and order like to hear how Robin and his Merry Men hoodwinked the Sheriff of Nottingham, and how Zorro beat the odds to make fools of the fat Spanish bureaucrats. Much is made of the good qualities of famous desperadoes. Such commonplace virtues as generosity, chivalry, and kindness to children and dogs have earned them far more credit than if they had been honest men.

While many an outlaw has carved himself a name in American folklore, it is the con man who is most admired in this country. Fast talking, wheeling and dealing, always on the move, he is as American as apple pie. If you have any doubts on this score, witness the popularity of J. R. on television's "Dallas" and the box-office success of *The Sting*.

As the term implies, the confidence artist gains the *confidence* of his victim in order to defraud him. The confidence game is theft through guile, usually in a one-on-one relationship. It is a widely held belief that the con artist makes out soley by cashing in on the larceny and greed inherent in human nature, a view which he happens to hold himself. He will tell you that you can't beat an honest man, and, in the same breath, that there is no such thing as an honest man.

According to the lore, the con artist is a pretty cool guy. Like our childhood hero Robin Hood, he lives by his wits, taking the rich and greedy for all they're worth. Unlike Robin Hood, however, he doesn't give away his booty to the poor. He just fleeces the bad guys and skates. He is assumed to be smart, perhaps a genius of sorts, with an intuitive understanding of his fellow man—and woman. He is smooth enough to charm the birds out of the trees. We want to identify with his success. The more outrageous his schemes, the more we laugh and the more we admire him.

But, for our own good, we shouldn't admire him too much. It is important to keep the stories separate from the facts, unless we want the last laugh to be on us. In which case, the con artist will be laughing, as the saying goes, all the way to the bank.

WHAT THE CON ARTIST IS REALLY LIKE

Any people I don't like I can hustle better.
Anonymous con man in an interview.
Richard H. Blum, *Deceivers and Deceived*

Although he enjoys socializing, the con man does not like

people much and actually holds a low opinion of humankind. His disrespect for his fellowman is coupled with an under-active conscience. What few twinges of conscience he may occasionally experience, he rationalizes away with the credo that the mark is snared by his own greed and dishonesty. And some of the time this is true.

Many times, however, it is neither greed nor dishonesty but some other human frailty, like loneliness, naiveté, or a soft heart, which he manipulates to bring about the mark's downfall. The con artist is not above using several different approaches until he hits on the one that works, provided he has time and thinks that it will be worth his while. Some-times he uses his considerable sales ability to outtalk some poor dupe until he or she becomes addled enough to sign the proffered contract or fork over Junior's college tuition, or both.

Whether the mark is a wealthy oil man or a senior citizen living on a scant fixed income, the con man has little sym-pathy for his mark's losses. He speaks happily of butchering, stripping, and beating his victims. When they complain he says they are squawking, bleating, or squealing. Even more than money, he loves the sense of conquest and power he derives from making others bend to his will.

Super Salesman

All of which is strange, because outwardly the con artist is such a nice guy: courteous, friendly, conventional, and nonthreatening. Easy to talk to, he is a super salesman and in fact is likely to hold legitimate or quasi-legitimate sales jobs from time to time. Those who have been gulled often say that he has a mesmerizing, or hypnotic, effect when he's into his pitch. If he appears to have an uncanny knack for seeing right through you to your innermost desires, don't be too impressed. He is assuming that your innermost desires are approximately the same as those of the rest of the population, and he goes from there, using any little clues or confessions you may blurt out to personalize his appeal. In so doing, the con man is just relying on time-tested techniques employed in high-pressure sales since business began.

The successful con artist is adept at using words, facial expressions, and body language to his own advantage; in other words, he knows how to charm as well as intimidate. And, of course, his freedom from conscience is a great boon to him in his work. However personal his line may seem, you are not the first person he has fed it to, nor will you be the last. Should you refuse to fall for it, he will keep trying until he finds someone who will, for, as the social scientists say, the con man is characteristically impervious to slight. To put it another way, his skin is as thick as a rhino's. Still, he will gladly pretend his feelings are hurt if he thinks he can sell you on his scam by making *you* feel guilty! It's all part of the sales pitch.

Great Pretender

Like many a good salesman, the con artist is also an actor. He enjoys impersonation, multiple identities, and costume to suit the occasion. He is ready to assume any role as long as he thinks there is profit in it, but his favorite is typically that of the big spender, the smooth dude with money to burn. Dressed to the hilt, he is prone to flashing fifty-dollar bills like a drug dealer and driving a luxurious, expensive car when he can.

He proves his acting ability when he makes you think that you are the greatest thing since sliced bread and that he is concerned first and foremost with *your* best interests. Always suspect you are dealing with a con man when you are offered a deal that sounds too good to be true. The next step is usually a request for something from you to show your good faith. Don't be persuaded by a con artist's act when you see this pattern emerge, no matter how convincing he may be.

You may wonder how anyone could be stupid enough to hand over money up front to a stranger, but the fact is that a con artist can be very convincing indeed. So much so that he seems to believe in his own spiel; and to some extent he does. When he gets into his act, he is not always sure when fantasy leaves off and reality begins. The game makes him feel like a winner and provides a substitute for friendship and love, emotions the con man can fake more reliably than he can feel.

Unfortunately for his stooges, the act put on by the con artist gives the illusion of being more real than the real thing. This is why a con artist can sell a sharp guy like you the Brooklyn Bridge, swampland in Florida, or a 1973 two-door, black-over-cream Olds Cutlass for only $400—price open for negotiation.

A big, honest-looking, fifty-three-year-old man in Detroit allegedly sold the car described above for at least $100 less than what he paid for it. One prospective customer reported that the seller, a Mr. J. J. McGowan, was even willing to kick in a free set of brand-new tires. Assuming that the vehicle was in good condition, why was McGowan amenable to taking such a loss? For those in the market for a 1973 Olds Cutlass, the deal must have sounded like a bargain.

Well . . . there *was* actually a catch. What McGowan lost in profit, he made up in volume by selling the same car to five different people. First he advertised in the newspaper and received forty-two responses. The phone messages were taken by a woman, a stranger hired by McGowan. He then made arrangements to drive the car to the home of each prospective customer, showing it and delivering his sales pitch, but never divulging his own whereabouts. Described by many as a natural salesman, he was very agreeable to making a deal with a prospective customer, offering to lower his price for those who haggled. He asked only that the buyer give him a down payment to show good faith and allow him to make the final delivery later in the day so that he could complete the necessary paperwork.

Even a natural doesn't score every time. For the five buyers who plunked down deposits ranging from $23 to $200, thirty-seven turned him down for one reason or another. As we said, the con artist is impervious to slight, and McGowan was no exception. He kept trying until he had made five sales and would doubtless have continued working the scam but for the fact that the newspaper in which he had placed his ad blew the whistle on him. Tipped off by the squeals, squawks, and bleats of the people McGowan had burned, the editors published a warning. A detective sergeant who recognized him from some other petty grift got into the act, and so McGowan quit when he was ahead only $473. Twenty-three dollars of this sum he returned to a welfare mother who told him that it was all she had in the world. Which just goes to show that everyone, even a con artist, has a soft spot somewhere.

According to *Car and Driver* magazine, the detective sergeant was not successful in his attempts to bring McGowan to justice. There have been sightings of McGowan peddling seafood door-to-door and offering great deals on bulk sales— cash in advance.

The Many Faces of the Confidence Man

There are many different kinds of con games and many different kinds of con artists. If you have a mental picture of a confidence man, erase it! When the real thing appears at your door, favorite bar, or Wednesday night Bible class (he can turn up any time, any place), he probably will not fit your idea of a crook. The people who bought J. J.

McGowan's Olds Cutlass said that he didn't look like a con man. That's because they *thought* they knew what a con man looks like!

The con artist may be a man or a woman, well educated or semiliterate, old or young. There have been many cases cited in which a con man will disguise himself as an older man in order to gain a mark's trust. He may come from the ghetto, a wealthy suburb, New York City, or the cornfields of the Great American Heartland. He may come from your own hometown, or convince you that he does. He may be a panhandler, cardsharp, or businessman. And he may pretend to be a member of any group that he thinks you respect. Trying to identify a con man or woman on the basis of appearance will only get you into trouble. Concentrate instead on generalizations that frequently hold true and on learning to spot the techniques and methods typically used in scams.

This diversity extends to the line of work in which the con man engages. Not all are good enough to rate the label con *artist,* but sometimes even a small-time grifter gets lucky. Whatever his background and skill level, he has probably engaged in other illegal activities in the past and usually will continue to do so when necessary. He is rarely so particular as to restrict himself exclusively to the confidence game, although he considers it the crème de la crème of crime. He looks down on thieves and muggers who have to resort to force in order to make a buck. He feels superior because he lives by his wits, making other people *willingly* give him what he wants.

This sense of superiority in outsmarting others often results in compulsive scamming. The natural con man will resort to scams even when it would be more profitable to pursue more conventional avenues of endeavor. It is interesting to note that many such people are talented and intelligent, and apparently have everything going for them. While they take great glee in misleading their marks and taking dishonest shortcuts in their repeated attempts to "make it big," they often end up as failures in life. A con artist does, though, make it to the top occasionally by means of his wheeling and dealing. And occasionally he even stays there. More often than not, he can't resist taking one more gamble and blows everything he has built up. It is a strange contradiction in his nature that though his main interest in life is to outsmart the rest of the world, he seems unable to resist outsmarting himself. The expression "He's so sharp he'll cut himself" was coined to describe this personality type.

The con man's value system is as full of contradictions as exist in other aspects of his life. In this area, as in others, he is not what he appears to be. He may believe in God, or in honor among thieves, or in the sanctity of motherhood. He may attend church, or even preach in one. He may spout gospel like a pro, but rest assured that he will not allow his beliefs to get in the way of his business. There will be contradictions between his words and actions, but such discrepancies do not worry him. Here his lack of conscience comes to his rescue, rendering any moral or religious beliefs superfluous.

He is equally two-faced in regard to the law. While he may claim to be an upstanding citizen, he is careful to stay one step ahead of the authorities, literally and figuratively. By the time his scams are discovered, he has just left town. His mailing address is likely to be a post office box or general pickup. If he requires a business office, it is here today and gone tomorrow, as befits a fly-by-night operation. He eludes the law by relocating and changing the name of his business whenever necessary. He usually surfaces in areas with high population densities—big cities, crowded resorts, and the like—where he has a wide choice of prospective marks and a good chance of preserving his precious anonymity.

When he is caught, he is incredulous. How could some fool

of a cop outsmart a genius like him? As you may have guessed, the con artist looks down on law-enforcement officials (although he may have a "Support Your Local Police" sticker on the bumper of his car).

Your Buddy the Con Artist

The none-too-flattering portrait of the con artist sketched above is a shallow characterization, as is any general description of a type. If you are unfortunate enough to have a friend, lover, employee, or other close acquaintance with a bunco soul, however, you will know this person as a complicated individual, not easily seen through or categorized. You will recognize some of the traits discussed here; but your friend may not possess all of the identifying marks of a con artist, or may be adept at using a personality smokescreen to keep you from seeing his or her true motives.

The relationship you develop with a con artist often assumes enough importance to you that you prefer to ignore the fact that you are being used. This is the old "I wonder, but I really don't want to know" syndrome that is typical of the dynamics that exist between con artist and sucker.

The games played in a close relationship are different from those used in a stranger-to-stranger con, although the basic techniques still apply. The confidence game can be seen as a sort of seduction, and nowhere is this more evident than in the personal relationship, where the con artist can exploit his persuasive skills to the hilt.

We are not speaking here exclusively about sexual seduction. There are countless ways in which a bunco artist can manipulate a friend. His shamelessness in taking advantage of you allows him to pull your strings in a calculating manner and then sit back, see how you react, and experiment with a new tack. If you balk or complain, he will use any of a number of tricks he carries up his sleeve to bring you back under control. Guilt, sympathy, jealousy, and anger are a few of the emotions he will try to arouse in you.

Acting ability is a must in this, as in any other, type of con job. The con artist will demonstrate that he sees in you something special; he becomes a mirror in which only your best qualities are reflected. Because no one else is willing to perform this service, it is especially difficult for the mark to risk shattering this positive image of himself that the con man presents. You don't want to act in a way that your friend won't like; you are reluctant to look hard enough to see him for what he really is.

Eventually, though, the day will come when you can no longer deny the truth of the situation. When you are finally ready to stand up for your rights, be prepared for recriminations and a big sob story. To the con artist, the story is always the important thing. This is why, when you rebel, he will be sincerely surprised and hurt. Perhaps the most maddening part of the whole story is that he—or she—will never admit to having behaved badly. You will probably be remembered by your bunco buddy as the bad guy when you break off the relationship.

You must break it off, though, if you don't want to be repeatedly taken advantage of. Otherwise the pattern of victimization will reemerge time and time again. The friendship must be permanently severed, or you will act as host to your parasitic pal indefinitely. If you have ever been through this experience, you know how hard it is to break away from such a relationship. Getting rid of a con artist friend is about as difficult as kicking a heroin or cigarette habit.

The story of Frank Thomas and Johnny Mueller illustrates a typical example of a bunco friendship. Frank wouldn't have been vulnerable to someone like Johnny if he had been a happier man. But his wife, Sheila, moved out one day when he was at work framing a house in a Houston suburb. When he came home that night, he was astonished to find all of her belongings—and many of his own—packed up in boxes. A note on the refrigerator door read: "Back tomorrow to pick up my things. Sheila."

Frank was devastated, but he had his practical side, too, and he realized that he needed someone to help him out with the rent. He advertised for a roommate—no drugs, no pets— and took in the first person to ring his doorbell.

The new roommate's name was Johnny Mueller. He was a little guy, short and skinny, so Frank was surprised when he asked if he could get a job on the construction crew.

"Can you frame?" Frank asked doubtfully. Johnny assured him that he could. Frank was further convinced when Johnny added that he wouldn't be able to pay his share of the rent unless he found a job soon.

The first day on the job site went fine. Not only was Johnny a great framer—he even showed Frank some short-cuts—but he was also hilarious company at the roadhouse after work. As the hour grew late, his mood became serious. He listened intently as Frank talked about Sheila. He seemed somehow to understand.

"You're one hell of a guy," he said, as Frank paid for the last round. "You're too good for a woman like her." Johnny had a way of looking you in the eye when he spoke, and Frank could see he meant what he said. He felt lucky to have Johnny for a roommate.

As the days passed, however, things began to go downhill. It wasn't so bad when Johnny brought home the little mongrel pup or even that he didn't have the patience to housebreak it. But he had started leaving work early and turning in an exorbitant number of hours when it came time to reckon the weekly payroll. People at work were asking Frank to account for his roommate. When Frank confronted Johnny with reporting more hours than he had worked, Johnny got furious.

"Are you calling me a liar?" he stormed. But when Frank stuck to his guns, Johnny finally backed down and admitted that he had a drug problem.

"You've done a lot for me," he said, after recounting some sad stories about his early childhood. "And I won't let you down again."

Johnny's behavior improved for a time, but it wasn't long before he fell back into his old habits. Gambling and drug dealing at the house were not tolerated by Frank; Johnny would use every trick he knew to bring Frank around. When the tricks didn't work, he would cooperate for a while until he figured Frank's "bad mood" had blown over. During this time he kept Frank entertained with funny stories and, more important, listened to Frank whenever he wanted to talk about Sheila. "She's not good enough for a man like you," Johnny would always say. When he wasn't upset with Johnny over some flagrant dereliction, Frank thought that he was the best roommate he had ever had.

Things changed when Sheila came home as unexpectedly as she had left. She had lost her job and was feeling down and out; Frank was happy to get her back. He told Johnny to start looking for another place to live. Since Johnny never paid his share of the rent anyway, Frank saw no reason to keep him on as a roommate. But Johnny just couldn't get motivated to go apartment hunting—although, to hear him tell it, he did nothing else but look for new lodgings. Frank figured that as long as Johnny was hanging around anyway, he might as well try to lift Sheila's spirits. It worried him that she still seemed so depressed.

"Forget what I told you about Sheila," he told his roommate, "and do what you can to cheer her up. You're really funny when you're on a roll. She's OK, you know—just kind of mixed up."

Johnny agreed to do his best, saying that as long as he lived, he would never understand why a great guy like Frank would put up with a woman like Sheila. After all, she didn't appreciate just how great a guy she was married to. Sheila, for her part, made fun of Johnny when she and her husband were alone together. She couldn't stand him, she said. And she detested the dog.

"Oh, Johnny's all right, honey," Frank would reply.

The next time Sheila left, she took everything that wasn't nailed down, including Johnny. The only thing they seemed to forget was the dog. And, of course, Frank. Frank and the abandoned dog grew close, and Frank took to saying that he would never trust another human being as long as he lived.

You might figure that Frank had learned his lesson by now but, if so, you're wrong. It wasn't even a month before Johnny called the house, inquiring after the dog. He said that he was planning to pay Frank the rent money he owed, but was vague as to when and how. He also said that the whole incident with Sheila had been her fault.

"She left me, too," he said. "You were right about her from the beginning, but a woman like that is hard to resist. She's not good enough for a man like you."

Frank had made up his mind never to speak to Johnny again, but the temptation to talk about Sheila proved too much to resist. He grudgingly agreed to have a beer with Johnny, and the last I heard they were rooming together again.

BUNCO TRAITS: A SUMMARY

As Frank discovered in getting to know Johnny, a con artist can be a very complicated individual, difficult to get a handle on. The following list does not sum up the personality and lifestyle of every con artist, but rather outlines common bunco characteristics.

The con man or woman is typically:

- inclined to hold a low opinion of humankind, although this inclination is generally well hidden.
- charming and personable. A super salesman, he appears nonthreatening.
- persistent and thick-skinned. He won't let a little failure get in the way of eventual success.
- an actor, who can fake emotions better than he can feel them. His act seems realer than real because he half believes it himself.
- not exclusively a con artist. He has engaged in, and will continue to engage in, other businesses, both legal and illegal, especially sales.
- proud of his ability to outsmart others and expects others to try to outsmart him. He is a compulsive scammer.
- lacking in conscience.
- disrespectful of police and others in authority.
- on the move, changing residences and businesses frequently.
- fond of showing off and is a big spender.

2.

Who Can Be a Mark?

Ninety-nine percent of the people in the world are fools and the rest of us are in great danger of contagion.

Thornton Niven Wilder, *The Matchmaker*

Rare indeed is the individual who is immune to the wiles of confidence artists throughout his life. The mark is not necessarily greedy, dishonest, stupid, or naive. He may just be in the right place at the wrong time.

If you have been the victim of a swindle or con game, you can take heart in the fact that this does not automatically label you a born sucker. People are more vulnerable at certain times than at others. A recent death in the family, a raise at work, even a passing mood affects a person's judgment. Either by coincidence or design, a con man may have caught you at a weak moment.

The pitch used by the con man is also of great importance. You may be unable to pass up a bargain, or you may be concerned about a loved one's welfare. Whatever your deepest desire may be, rest assured that there is a charlatan out there somewhere willing to take advantage of it. Your friendly con artist will be only too happy to relieve you of your worries, not to mention a fair portion of your cash.

While victims of con games do not fall neatly into any one category, police reports indicate that the largest percentage of those who report bunco incidents have several characteristics in common. They tend to be middle class, narrow-minded, eager to please or to be thought of as "nice," poorly educated, and isolated.

On the other hand, those who consider themselves too smart to be taken in by a scam are sometimes fooled just as easily as the gullible. If you think that you can't fool the old fooler, remember the saying, "No one gets conned like the con man." An appeal to one's worldliness, obvious street wisdom, and superior intelligence, coupled with an offer of easy money, will often do the trick.

HOW LIKELY ARE YOU TO BECOME A MARK?

Even if you have none of the characteristics mentioned above, you can still be a bunco target; there will be times when you are unusually prone to swallow the con man's line. Take the test below to see how vulnerable you are at this particular point in your life. Your total score is less important than what you discover about yourself.

1. Have you moved recently, or are you away from your own turf?
2. Have you been divorced or widowed within the last two years?
3. Have you become a member of the armed forces within the last two years?
4. Have you lost touch with close friends or family?
5. Would you call yourself a loner?
6. Would you describe yourself as "very religious"?
7. Do you assume that people in general are honest?
8. Do you try to follow the letter of the law in all things?

9. Do you believe there is no excuse for acting discourteously, especially to guests?
10. In making an important decision, would you take the word of an expert instead of checking for yourself?
11. Do you often think what you should have said after it's too late?
12. Do you place importance on what others, even strangers, think of you?
13. Are you easily hypnotized?
14. Do you follow your horoscope regularly and take it to heart?
15. Do you believe psychics or fortune-tellers to be so reliable that you base your actions on their advice?
16. Do you try a lot of health fads—everything from natural foods to rolfing?
17. Do you send away for remedies, cures, and opportunities advertised in magazines?
18. Do you answer chain letters and send in money?
19. Do you strike up friendships quickly—and sometimes wish you hadn't?
20. Do you gamble?
21. Do you think you're too smart to be conned?
22. Are you so impatient with details that you act impulsively?
23. Is it hard to resist free gifts, garage sales, bargains, get-rich-quick schemes?
24. Do you figure that some day you'll get lucky and make your fortune?
25. Do you assume that everyone is out for himself; that anyone would be dishonest if he thought he could get away with it?

The way you answer the questionnaire cannot predict with absolute accuracy your chances of getting taken by a con artist. It *can*, however, point out your vulnerable areas, assuming you have any, and give you an idea of what you need to look out for. "Yes" answers imply susceptibility.

New Kid in Town

The first five questions deal more with the stress in your daily life than with your personality. You might answer "yes" to all five questions and still be impervious to the wiles of a con artist. But these outside influences can, and often do, make a difference in the way an individual reacts to others.

Questions 1 through 3 pertain to changes in lifestyle, habits, and environment. Any recent, abrupt life change can alter your sense of balance and, therefore, your judgment. If you have gone through a serious upheaval, you know that your thinking—and most likely your behavior—was different than usual, if only for a time. Cons are aware of such changes, and make a point of establishing contact with widows, widowers, tourists, travelers, divorcees, and young servicemen. Those away from home or separated from loved ones are attractive targets for finaglers of all types.

Question 4, "Have you lost touch with close friends or family?" is important for two reasons. First, a person who answers "yes" may well be lonely, ready to go along with any friendly, fast-talking stranger. Second, such a person is likely to make decisions on impulse, under the influence of the con, without consulting people he can trust. When it becomes apparent that a mark is contacting friends or family partway through a scam, a con will often drop the whole business and seek out other prey.

If you answered "yes" to question 5, you should realize that you may be a target of sharpers when you go out on your own—unless, of course, you resemble Mr. T, a Hell's Angel, or a prominent mobster, in which case you will probably be left alone. (Couples are also sometimes hit on if they look as if they are still in the get-acquainted phase because the con man can play on their desire to impress one another. Con men usually consider couples and tight groups to be poor risks.)

Dudley Do-Right

Affirmative answers to questions 6 through 8 establish you as a straight person. Being straight does not automatically qualify you as a sucker, and not all suckers are straight. (Al Capone was no Sunday school teacher, yet he gave Victor Lustig, a Czech famous for twice selling the Eiffel Tower, $50,000 to invest for him on the assurance that he would double his investment on Wall Street within two months! Lustig voluntarily returned the money soon afterward, however.)

When religious, law-abiding folk become isolated, their own conformity to rules often blinds them to the fact that not everyone thinks or behaves as they do. Such people can be easy pickings for the unprincipled. Their readiness to assume that others are as good as they are is encouraged by the con artist, who will put on a show to assure them that he is one of the flock. The mark's exaggerated respect for authority also plays an important role here.

Number 9, "Do you believe that there is no excuse for acting discourteously, especially to guests?" is a key question. Many people act on this belief, and con men and other high-pressure salesmen routinely use a mark's good manners against him. True, the bunco salesperson who has forced his or her way into your home is not, strictly speaking, a guest, but once the intruder is there, you may feel obligated to extend hospitality. Don't fall for this trick! Don't allow strangers into your house. If one does get in and proceeds to try to run a number on you, treat him like any other vermin that gains entrance from time to time and get rid of him. Threaten to call the police if necessary. You don't have to be polite.

Polite people also labor under another disadvantage: They unconsciously ignore signals that others are lying, because they know it would be discourteous to call attention to, or even to observe, these signals. Other, less polite, people may also overlook these signals simply because they are not tuned in to them. Psychologist Paul Ekman, author of *Telling Lies*, has made an eighteen-year study of liars and offers the following suggestions.

- Professional liars, like performers and diplomats (and con artists) are the most difficult to read. Still, even the best may slip up sometimes. Those practiced at lying tend to control their facial muscles better than their voices or body language. Therefore, if you suspect that you are being conned, watch for gestures instead of concentrating on the face. Shrugging one shoulder, and other ambivalent gestures, can give away a prevaricator. The speaker who customarily gestures a lot, then suddenly stops all gesturing, is often lying.

- Some facial expressions are nearly impossible to fake. In a true grieving expression, the upper eyelids and inner eyebrow corners pull up. Most people cannot act this out correctly (although Woody Allen's "mask of grief" is his trademark). In an expression of fear or worry, the eyebrows rise and draw together. This expression also is rarely feigned correctly. Unless a person has a naturally crooked smile, an assymetrical smiling expression is usually a sign of lying. (Remember Eddy Haskell of "Leave It to Beaver" fame?)

- Beware when a smile, look of astonishment, or other facial expression lasts longer than four or five seconds. Generally, real expressions of emotion change quickly. Another warning sign: an emotional gesture and facial expression that either do not agree or are out of sync with one another.

- Those who need practice in recognizing a lie when they

hear one might conduct their own exercise, observing what they know to be natural signs of various emotional states and then contrasting them with faked expressions and gestures. Keep in mind that a shy and insecure person often looks as if he is lying when he is actually telling the truth, just as professional liars often betray no emotion at all or appear to be sincere when they're lying! It's a tricky business, but with practice you can improve your ratio of right to wrong guesses.

Question 10 indicates whether you prefer to do your own thinking or to let someone else do your thinking for you. There are times when you must take someone else's word, and you can't be an expert in every field. When you routinely assume, however, that "they know better than I do," you are in danger of becoming someone's pigeon. It follows that any time you put up money for any purpose, you should be certain that you understand the deal completely. Studies have shown that victims of con games often don't mind being confused, but are comfortable in letting others handle everything for them. They relinquish control of the situation by not insisting that details be clear before they pay. *Read the small print, ask questions, and take your time.* A trustworthy salesperson, broker, banker, or other professional will not try to rush you into signing away your savings in a whirlwind of excitement. If you are told that you have to act fast and there is no time for calm deliberation or to get other opinions, forget it. It is a con man's tactic to rush clients into quick decisions. Contact the Better Business Bureau or your state attorney general when you question a company's legitimacy.

If you answered "yes" to question 11, join the crowd. This is a common response. In dealing with a con artist, however, realizing what you should have said after the fact doesn't cut it. You need to keep your wits about you. It isn't necessary that you try to follow his patter, think as fast as he, or outtalk him. In fact, doing so can even get you into trouble; it's listening to the small voice deep inside you screaming "fake! fake!" and acting on your gut reaction that saves you from being conned. Your intuition will probably tell you that something is amiss; the smooth operator will probably attempt to override your intuitive objections with self-serving logic and carefully selected "facts" and statistics. Stick to your guns, but don't bother to argue. That's what he wants you to do. (A con artist in a debate is as much at home as B'rer Rabbit in the briar patch.) All you have to say is "no." What if you don't say "no" and later wish you had? In home solicitation sales, the salesman is required by law to inform you of your three-day right to cancel any contract or agreement you sign. If he doesn't inform you of this right, or if he refuses to honor it, notify the Federal Trade Commission and the local police. Any money you have already put into a con man's hand, however, will be difficult—if not impossible—to recover.

Everyone likes to be liked. But if you answered question 12 in the affirmative and also have two or more "yes" answers to questions 13 through 19, you must guard carefully against being victimized. Caring too much what others think is a habit that will play you right into a con man's hands. The person who wants to be thought of as nice, a good sport, or a likable guy is at a serious disadvantage with someone who knows how to manipulate him. If you are also a trusting soul, you stand to lose out in a confrontation with a sharper.

Starry-Eyed Innocent

Questions 13 through 19 deal with gullibility. Most people are gullible because they believe what they want to believe. Someone clever enough to present an attractive story can make out as a result. Some people want so much to put faith in a remedy, get-rich-quick scheme, or romance that they are willing to risk playing the fool over and over again in the hope that next time the pie in the sky will be theirs.

Question 13, "Are you easily hypnotized?" is important, although not everyone who can be hypnotized is a natural sucker. Some people who allow themselves to be hypnotized easily are especially suggestible. They submit to someone else's will, allowing that person to guide and influence them more than is wise. Those who have been taken in by con men often say that they were "mesmerized" or "hypnotized"; to those open to suggestion, the con man seems to weave a spell.

Successful salesmen, preachers, lawyers, and others whose livelihood depends on the ability to persuade others use techniques similar to those of the professional hypnotist. So do confidence artists. If you get the feeling you are being swayed by a convincing speaker and don't know why, ask yourself whether he is using the following hypnotic techniques.

- Pacing. A persuasive speaker *paces* his speaking voice, posture, and gestures to your mood, behavior, speech, and experience. He may even adopt your accent and use your slang. In other words, he takes his cues from you and offers you a reflection of yourself. His subtle implication is that you and he are on the same wavelength. He makes bland, obviously truthful statements about the weather, traffic, or whatever so that you get used to believing what he says. Pacing makes you trust the speaker. If you object to something the speaker proposes, he agrees, taking away your grounds for resistance.

- Command. Beware the speaker who makes liberal use of your first name! This is a common ploy used to influence you subliminally. The speaker will weave a *command* into an apparently innocuous remark, looking you in the eye and saying your name for emphasis so that the command sinks in.

- Story-telling. As the eminent anthropologist Gregory Bateson has observed, human beings think in terms of stories. This is true no matter how rational and fact-oriented they may be in their business dealings. When a speaker works his pitch into a story, the listener will pick up and remember it better than he would absorb a barrage of statistics. The story format has another advantage in that it is an indirect, nonchallenging way to relay information. While you might question a statement offered as fact, you are less likely to argue with an anecdote. Thus the speaker influences you in a round-about way.

As for questions 14 through 18: We are not denying that there is never any value in astrology, fortune-telling, health foods, and "alternative medicine" cures of the sort advertised in the back pages of magazines, or that there is any great harm in indulging in a chain letter now and again. The point is that those who habitually place their faith in such things are just the sort of passive, trusting folk the con artist is happiest to meet. Horoscopes can be fun, a visit to Lady Estella may be enlightening, and maybe it serves you right to get rolfed. But remember that you are in charge of your own destiny and are ultimately responsible for what happens to you. Don't hand over the controls to the first turbaned swami who strolls your way. (And, by the way, if you want to make money on a chain letter, you have to be the one who starts it.)

The reason for the inclusion of question 19, "Do you strike up friendships easily?" is simple: The con artist cannot ensnare a mark without first establishing contact. Guarded, reserved, shy, or snobbish people have fewer friends than those more receptive to the overtures of strangers, but they also get conned less.

Wild and Crazy Guy

Those who answer "yes" to three of the last six questions

belong to a class of easy marks who may know better at every stage of the game, but who can't resist playing anyway. Cons look for gamblers, knowing that those willing to take risks on a long shot are more apt to go for it than their cautious brethren. The gambler knows he's not likely to get rich through diligence and hard work, but he just *might* luck out by means of a contest, lottery, or scam. Besides, such a person finds a con artist very entertaining company and may string along with him just to see what comes next. He may go along with a con artist purely out of admiration for his style.

People who think they are too smart to be conned are often victimized through their own greed. They are not trusting, but when the con artist offers them a no-risk, illegal deal, they go for it. After all, they figure, that's the way the world operates. All the fat cats got their money by scamming, so why shouldn't they? In their haste to make a quick and easy buck, they lose sight of the fact that, if a deal sounds too good to be true, it probably is. The con artist himself is a classic example of this personality type.

CONNING THE MORMONS IN SALT LAKE CITY

No discussion of confidence-game marks would be complete without mentioning the Mormons of Salt Lake City. Just as Florida is renowned for its boiler-room operators and land-sale swindlers and New York City is notorious for its muggers, Utah is famous for its easy marks.

At least nine thousand inhabitants of Salt Lake City, whose population is reckoned to be at least 70 percent Mormon, have been victims of swindled investment confidence scams during the last few years. Investors have lost over $200 million as a result.

But why? Members of the Church of Jesus Christ of Latter Day Saints—commonly known as Mormons—are pragmatic survivalists. They aren't any greedier than anyone else and are demonstrably less larcenous than the norm. There is certainly no evidence that they are stupid. It is probably the Latter-Day Saints' respect for their clergymen, combined with a healthy regard for American capitalism, that is at the root of their propensity for victimization.

Approached by well-respected community and church members with opportunities to enrich the church, several lay preachers gladly invested and encouraged their congregations to do the same. The clergymen had no inkling that the investment schemes were not on the up-and-up, and their congregations, used to accepting church counsel on spiritual matters, now accepted advice on financial matters just as willingly. If the preacher said yea, who were they to say nay?

Most of the scammers who fleeced the flocks were no strangers to the community. Take, for example, Veldon Taylor, owner of T&D Management. He had an AAA rating with the BBB (Better Business Bureau), and his sales staff pitched pork bellies and other commodities at local Mormon ward meetings. He promised investors 30 percent a year for their money; what reason did the good people have to suspect him? Veldon Taylor came out of the deal with $4 million. His investors emerged without their shirts.

Another fraud involved Grant Affleck, church member in good standing and head of Afco, a major real estate development company in the Salt Lake City area. The fact that Afco was deeply in debt was not common knowledge. Most people believed that the company was not only solvent, but prospering, and Affleck certainly did everything in his power to foster this misconception.

In collaboration with a finance company, Affleck convinced home owners to take out second mortgages on their houses and then lend the cash to Afco. Afco would service the mortgage, paying interest, which at that time was running about 20 percent on a second mortgage. Afco would also pay the home owner 10 percent of the mortgage loan amount.

Approximately two thousand people fell for Affleck's second-mortgage scam. All told, Affleck relieved his good neighbors in Salt Lake City of more than $20 million.

Among the many swindles and frauds that plagued the Mormon community was a proliferation of Ponzi schemes. A Ponzi operator offers a so-called investment opportunity and promises a high yield within a short period of time. Monies taken in are never put into the project as advertised, but are used, pyramid-style, to pay earlier investors. Original participants are paid the promised return amount—and sometimes more—to encourage them to tell their friends about the great deal they have received. To keep going, a Ponzi operation must enlist increasingly large numbers of investors. Eventually this becomes impossible, and the structure collapses, leaving participants in the lurch. In the Independent Clearing House scam, which operated in forty states but fleeced more than its fair share of lambs in Salt Lake City, it has been said that mastermind Richard Cardell, Sr., planned the entire sequence of events, including the use of Chapter 11 (bankruptcy filing) as a means to end the operation.

Ironically, the very qualities that distinguish the Latter-Day Saints as fine, upstanding citizens proved to be their financial downfall at the hands of con artists. Because they were religious, law-abiding, and community- and church-oriented, they tended to be sheltered and trusting. They took the word of those they looked up to in the community hierarchy—lay preachers, bank officers, and well-heeled businessmen—rather than researching the facts for themselves. Officials of the Church of Jesus Christ of Latter-Day Saints have issued warnings to church members, but Utah remains a prime hunting ground for many a bunco artist.

Says Frederick A. Moreton, a vice-president of Kidder, Peabody & Co. in Salt Lake City: "If it works in California or Colorado, it's bound to work in Utah."

3.

It's a Living

We are errant knaves, all; believe none of us.
William Shakespeare, *Hamlet*

Though all con artists have certain elements in common—larceny in the heart, for example—they differ widely in personal style and types of cons they perpetrate. Some specialize in one bunco area, while others are general practitioners in the field of con game artistry. The following stories are true, allowing for some slight exaggeration in those cases in which the source of the anecdote is the con man himself!

THE TICHBORNE CLAIMANT

One of England's most unlikely imposters was Arthur Orton, a fat commoner from a large, poverty-stricken family in London, who emigrated to Australia in 1852. He settled in Wagga Wagga, where he became a cattle slaughterer. In 1865 he read an advertisement which gave him the idea to go back to England and attempt to pass himself off as the son and heir of the fabulously wealthy Lady Tichborne. But, wait, we are getting ahead of ourselves here.

The story really begins with the young Sir Roger Charles Doughty Tichborne and his hopeless love for his cousin. Sir

Roger, heir to his family fortune, was a soldier with a commission in the Sixth Dragoon Guards. He was, unfortunately, in love with his first cousin, Katherine Doughty, whom he was forbidden to marry, and the frustration of the situation was driving him crazy. He felt he had to get out of England, and his mother agreed. (It was thought that a long sea voyage would put the lovely relative out of his mind.) Sir Roger resigned his commission and set off in a small sailing ship for South America. From Rio de Janeiro, the ship once again set sail, this time for New York, and that was the last anyone ever heard of the young aristocrat. The ship's log book was eventually found, four hundred miles out to sea; otherwise there was no trace of Sir Roger or his ship, the *Bella*.

As is typical of mothers the world over, Lady Tichborne refused to believe the worst. Over the years, she kept hoping that one day Sir Roger would return, safe and sound, from some exotic outpost of the Empire and resume his position as scion of the Tichborne estate. To this end, she placed advertisements in newspapers around the world for news of her son. When Lord Tichborne, her husband, died, she clung even more resolutely to her belief that her eldest son would come home.

Twelve years after Sir Roger's disappearance, Lady Tichborne received a letter from Australia that made her rejoice. It was from her son, who had been shipwrecked but was now able to return to his rightful estate, bringing a wife and baby girl!

Eager to see her long-lost son, Lady Tichborne was ready to agree to anything and acceded to Roger's rather eccentric wish that their reunion take place in a darkened room. When her "son" spoke of his military service in the ranks (Sir Roger, remember, was a commissioned officer) and his school days at Winchester (an institution which Sir Roger had never attended), when he forgot his French and reminisced about his dear old grandad (who had died before Roger's birth),

Lady Tichborne merely sighed. "He confuses everything, as in a dream," she said.

The rest of the family was less accepting; the man was obviously an imposter. For one thing, anyone could see that this fat, red-faced mountain of a man was not their Roger. Roger had been slender, slight, and pale. And Roger had had a tattoo on his arm; this man had none. Even if it were possible that Sir Roger had so drastically changed his appearance, personality, and accent during his twelve-year absence, surely he would remember something about his family, school, and professional life. Lady Tichborne refused to be put off by her family's warnings. To their disgust, she immediately gave the claimant a generous allowance and had him installed in the mansion.

The claimant was, of course, not Sir Roger at all, but Arthur Orton. His outrageous nerve had paid off, and he was finally as wealthy and secure as he had ever dreamed of being when he was Down Under in Wagga Wagga. Never mind the snubs of the Tichbornes or the old family servants. He and his wife and daughter were set for life; his descendents would inherit the Tichborne title. But, he began to think, it wasn't really fair that he wouldn't inherit more. As eldest son, the family fortune was also his due. Yet on Sir Tichborne's death, the fortune had passed to Alfred, Roger's younger brother. Alfred had also died, and his baby son, Henry, had received Roger's rightful inheritance.

The more Orton considered this, the angrier it made him. He began to prepare a legal case against Henry and his interests. It took him five years to prepare for the trial, during which time he researched family history, befriended men from Sir Roger's regiment in the Sixth Dragoon Guards, and lined up one hundred witnesses who would swear in court that he was indeed Sir Roger. It is interesting to conjecture whether these witnesses could possibly have been fooled by Orton, or whether they were bribed with the promise of sharing the wealth when Orton won his case against little Henry.

Lady Tichborne died shortly before the trial date, and Orton thus lost his ace in the hole. Nevertheless, his one hundred witnesses duly testified on his behalf, swearing that Orton was Sir Roger. The family was able to round up only seventeen witnesses to deny his claim.

The trial, which had begun on 11 May 1871, ran on for 103 days. Despite his witnesses and exhaustive research, Orton was not able to convince the court that he was the missing heir; numerous inconsistencies undermined his story. At the end of the trial, Orton was immediately taken into custody as an impostor and charged with perjury. A new trial was scheduled, this time with Orton as defendant, and Orton was found guilty of perjury and sentenced to fourteen years in prison. Upon his release ten years later, he immediately renewed his claim on the Tichborne estate, but nothing came of it. Orton died a pauper in 1898.

FOLK HERO FORGER

In December 1984, Edgar Derube, then twenty-six, was arrested in Boulder, Colorado. He had been working in a local seafood restaurant, posing as Peter Kern, a member of the wealthy Kern Foods family, since his escape from the New Hampshire State Prison some weeks earlier. Derube, according to prosecutors, had become a folk hero for faking his way out of the prison with forged papers.

None of this was unusual for Derube, who became an accomplished forger and imposter very early in life. To facilitate past scams, he successfully passed himself off as an American blueblood, occasionally impersonating children and grandchildren of the Kennedy, du Pont, and other wealthy families.

Upon his arrest, Derube told a federal magistrate in Denver that he wanted to waive extradition and be returned to New

Hampshire as soon as possible. "I'd like to clear this up," he said innocently. "It's all a big mess."

CHECKERED CAREER OF
FRANK ABAGNALE

Frank Abagnale started his life of crime by conning his own doting father at the age of fifteen. He took up bunco partly as a means of financing his favorite hobby—womanizing—and partly just for the challenge of the game. Abagnale, by his own account, enjoyed the thrill of winning even more than the luxuries he gleaned from his confidence tricks.

In 1964, as Dr. Frank Williams, pediatrician, he conned the staff of a Georgia children's hospital into hiring him as a specialist. He read everything he could on children's diseases and was sure to consult other doctors on their opinions before making a diagnosis. Growing nervous, "Williams" eventually left his staff position of his own free will. He was not exposed as a fraud, although he worked at the hospital, earning excellent money, for nearly a year.

Abagnale then forged himself a degree from Harvard Law School and became Robert Conrad. He practiced law for nine months, but finally quit the profession when a colleague began to grow suspicious.

As Frank Adams, Ph.D., Abagnale taught sociology at a Utah College. This was hardly enough of a challenge, however, so he gave up his post after only three months.

As an airline pilot he surpassed himself, although he flew only on a standby basis. He had papers forged by printers who never questioned his reasons for needing such authorization. And he found that wearing a uniform put him above suspicion; women and children smiled at him, and everyone seemed respectful, helpful—and trusting. It was an excellent disguise. Flirting with an attractive stewardess in flight one day, he saw that a great opportunity was about to present itself. The stewardess had forgotten to cash her paycheck and had no cash. Soon the plane would be landing in Mexico, and she was uncertain whether the hotel would be willing to honor her check. Abagnale gladly took it and paid her in cash. He never even cashed her check later. The company check was to prove extremely useful to him in his sideline of forgery and bad-check passing. (Over a five-year period, he professedly cashed over $2.5 million in bad checks.)

At an Acapulco hotel, after snowing the manager, he confidentially admitted that he had left the States without his passport, bringing only a visa. Now, he said, he had been assigned to fly to England and lacked the necessary papers to enter that country. "What am I gonna do, Pete?" he asked. "If the super learns I'm here without a passport, he'll fire me."

The manager happened to know some people who were able to obtain a fake passport for "Captain Frank Williams"— and Abagnale had another valuable piece of I.D.

In 1971 Abagnale was lying low in the French countryside, living under one of his many pseudonyms, when he was nabbed by detectives who had been on his trail for months, due to a banking "indiscretion" on Abagnale's part. His career now at an end, he was convicted of fraud and sentenced to prison in France, after which he was sent to Sweden to be tried for crimes in that country. After serving his time in Sweden, he was flown back to the United States, where he was also wanted for various frauds, forgeries, and swindles. . . . All in all, Abagnale spent five years behind bars.

Abagnale now spends his days giving seminars to bankers and merchants on how to detect con men and their schemes. He says publicly that he has gone straight, though some wonder whether a con man can ever completely eradicate the larceny in his heart.

ARTHUR LEE TROTTER,
SPORTS STAR IMPERSONATOR

Since 1954, Arthur Lee Trotter has been arrested twenty-three times, usually on charges of fraud, forgery, and impersonation. He is not content to impersonate just anybody, though. Trotter has always wanted to be a sports star. During one of his more recent arrests, Trotter was pretending to be Bill Russell, former center for the Boston Celtics. He was also pretending to sell a woman a $2,500 share in a restaurant chain. Both pretenses were bogus, and the woman, who already had her suspicions, alerted the police.

Officers hidden in the next room listened to the conversation between Trotter and the woman. She told Trotter that he didn't look like Bill Russell, who was much taller. Trotter ad-libbed that he had been in a car accident and had undergone surgery. Warming to his role, he added that he had become tired of "having my legs hang off of motel beds," and also "wanted to fit easier into my new Mercedes." He therefore decided to have ten inches of shinbone removed from each leg.

The police escorted Trotter to the Natchitoches, Louisiana, station house, where he abruptly changed his tune. No, he wasn't Bill Russell, he confessed; in reality he was Marv Fleming, former tight end with the Green Bay Packers. To prove it, he produced a falsified driver's license, insurance policies, and personal checks. In the trunk of his car were photographs of himself brandishing Packers and Dolphins jerseys with Fleming's number on them. The police were inclined to believe him, but decided to check by calling Fleming's residence in California.

Fleming had had trouble with Trotter before. On one occasion, he received a bill from an Oakland, California, motel. At the time the bill was run up, he had been in

Europe. Another time, he received a letter from a woman in Oakland informing him that his baby had been born. He called the woman and broke the news to her that he wasn't the dad. Trotter also used Fleming's identity in Tyler, Texas, where he was arrested for selling fake stock in NFL teams. Just outside Tyler, he gave an interview to a high-school paper while posing as Fleming. He also dated a Tyler high-school girl under false pretenses. Until she heard of Trotter's arrest in Louisiana, she later said, she had always believed that he actually was Marv Fleming.

When Trotter was visited in jail by reporters, he admitted that his affairs might seem pretty mixed up, but said that when his lawyer, "Melvin Belli," arrived, everything would be clear.

The real Marv Fleming has stated that he couldn't believe anyone would fall for Trotter's impersonation. Fleming, now an actor, is by his own admission handsome, with perfect teeth; Trotter is fat, "pig-ugly," and has crooked teeth.

JOE FLYNN, "THE STINGMAN"

For London's *Time Out* magazine, con artist Joe Flynn came briefly out of hiding in order to "set the record straight" and perhaps to boast a little as well. *Time Out* staff checked out his all-but-unbelievable stories and found that, for once, Flynn was telling the truth.

Joe Flynn is about fifty now and semiretired, living a secluded and secretive life in the south of France. He calls himself a *stingman,* and feels he is more successful than most being that he has spent very little time behind bars. Flynn has put on some weight since his younger, flashier days as a general practitioner of the grift. His specialty has been impersonation for the purpose of extracting money from publishers, businessmen—including John De Lorean—and bankers, as well as the FBI, CIA, and various embassies. Flynn has said he still keeps his hand in by constantly reading up on current events in order to get leads for scams. By doing his homework, he is also able to skim off those small details that lend an air of authenticity to an otherwise completely fabricated story.

Flynn has conned many a mark in this day, but perhaps never so gleefully as when he was pulling the wool over Rupert Murdoch's eyes. What started out as a vendetta against Murdoch's father—also a newspaper publisher—in Sydney, Australia, many years ago has grown into a pleasurable pastime for the con man. Apparently, when Flynn complained to the elder Murdoch about the tardy placement of a classified ad in one of his papers, the publisher was rude and unaccommodating. Because the ad was placed late, Flynn lost money on a real-estate option; to then have his complaint discourteously brushed off was too much. Flynn swore revenge.

Murdoch frustrated Flynn further, though, by dying before the revenge could be exacted. As it turned out, this proved to be no problem; Flynn simply took it out on Rupert Murdoch, the old man's son. At one time he got $37,000 from Murdoch for a pair of old shoes supposedly last worn by Jimmy Hoffa. Flynn had picked them up at the Salvation Army.

Joe was born Barry Gray in Camberwell, South London, the son of a chorus girl. His father, whom he describes as a "professional dance partner," didn't stay around long, and mother and child traveled the country playing the music halls. He learned from his mother how to make money in a pinch and also picked up acting skills which would stand him in good stead later in life. Much of his childhood was spent backstage, and he lived in a world of make-believe.

After a stint in the RAF and a short career in the Merchant Marines, Joe Flynn jumped ship in Sydney, Australia; he was not yet twenty-one. There he slipped naturally and easily into con artistry. Selling refrigerators, floor polish, and portable outhouses door-to-door in little towns in Tasmania suited Flynn. He used every trick in the book to pitch his wares and signed up buyers on time payments. To sell the portable outhouses, he had his sales teams wear white coats with "HEALTH DEPARTMENT" stenciled across the back. Flynn, of course, had no connection with the health department, but the coats seemed to make the buyers feel more secure.

Door-to-door sales were just the beginning for Flynn, whose interest soon turned to the real estate business. With a beautiful blonde named Vivien, he went into the vacation-home business, pushing holiday flats in Costa Brava, Spain, through a London office. The business, called Properties Espanol, prospered in the early 1960s, although the properties were falsely advertised and were not what the tourists had been led to expect. When Joe and Vivien decided it was time to go back to Australia, they packed up eighteen deposits, totaling about £20,000, and split.

Flynn continued his real estate career in Australia. A fast-talker and compulsive gambler, both at the tables and in his business, he quickly built up a paper empire, based on second mortgages, loan capital, and Ponzi operations—taking from Peter to pay Paul. Generous and flamboyant, Flynn took friends on all-expense-paid vacations around the South Seas and donated heavily to the local liberal party. (At one time he even met Prime Minister Malcom Fraser.) During this period he lavished expensive jewelry on Vivien, his partner in countless stings. Although Flynn was a ladies' man, he was loyal in his way to Vivien, and they maintained their relationship over twenty years of chicanery.

When Flynn's paper empire collapsed in the mid-Seventies, he expeditiously left Australia with $27,000 in his pocket overdrawn from eight separate bank accounts . By this time his name had changed so many times that Flynn himself had difficulty remembering his true identity. Now he was once again changing his name, life, and business, at the age of forty-two.

Flynn returned to Australia shortly afterward, staying only long enough to reclaim the jewelry he had showered on Vivien, thereby severing their relationship. On the flight back to England, Flynn happened to find an out-dated magazine containing an article about Teamster boss Jimmy Hoffa, written three weeks before he disappeared. He read the article and saved it for future reference. From a London apartment, he began putting together a scam to replenish his funds. He would pose as an informant who knew what had happened to Hoffa, but who was afraid for his life and must therefore resort to clandestine means of operation. After a false lead or two, he contacted Rupert Murdoch, owner of the *New York Post*, the *Village Voice*, *New York* magazine, the *Boston Herald*, the *Chicago Sun-Times*, and London's *News of the World*, among other publications. Flynn convinced Murdoch that he had valuable information to sell, then hit up the publisher for $2,000 to get to Las Vegas. "That's where a lot of my contacts start," Flynn explained. Murdoch had an employee bring the money to Southampton by train and leave it with a friend of Flynn's. Flynn picked it up, flew to Vegas, and promptly blew it on the tables.

He then got back in touch with Murdoch, who was now in Adelaide, Australia. Flynn was careful to reverse the charges for his phone call. He explained that he needed $8,000 to pay for more information from people who were reluctant to talk. Murdoch had Flynn fly to Los Angeles. A friend chauffered Flynn in a Cadillac to an agreed-upon location, where a contact threw a package of bills into his lap. Flynn paid his driver $1,000, flew back to Las Vegas, and blew the balance gambling.

Flynn needed more cash, but figured that he had to have

something to keep up Murdoch's interest. So he went to a thrift store and bought a pair of shoes, guessing the size from the physical description of Hoffa in the magazine article. Then he phoned the publisher with the news that he had found the man who had dumped Hoffa; he was hiding in Germany, and had saved the shoes as security in case someone tried to kill him. He would deliver the shoes as proof, but needed $20,000 and $5,000 in expenses.

Murdoch sent his right-hand man to Cologne, Germany, with a check for $22,000 to be cashed in a German bank and $5,000 cash, which was handed over to a friend of Flynn's known as the Dutchman at a Holiday Inn near the airport. In return, the Dutchman gave the contact a key to an airport locker which contained the shoes. Flynn melted away into the background, leaving Murdoch to wonder what had happened to his informant.

In 1983, Flynn hit Murdoch again, this time through former journalist of the year John Swain, who was writing for Murdoch's *Sunday Times*. Posing as an IRA informer, he told Swain how he had helped Palestine terrorists to flee France, supplying Carlos the Jackal with a passport. The two met in Paris; Swain gave Flynn 5,000 francs and set up a future meeting in County Cork, Ireland. (Flynn didn't show up.)

To practice for the role of IRA informant, Flynn not only read up on his current events, but also mentally lived the role of "Mr. Patrick, the Irishman." For ten hours before his interview with Swain, Flynn spoke to himself like an Irishman in his hotel room. (Flynn uses his boyhood experience in the theaters to act out his roles so that he even believes them himself, at least for the moment. "When I go in," he told *Time Out*, "I am what I am until we part.")

Once again doing his *yacka* (Australian for homework), Flynn discovered that De Lorean was suing London's *Daily Mirror* for its insinuation that funds were being channeled out of De Lorean's automobile company in Belfast, Northern

Ireland, into a Swiss bank account. Flynn knew from his reading that the *Mirror*'s editorial stance was decidedly anti-De Lorean. Shrewdly figuring that the editors of the publication would like nothing better than to get some straight dope to support their position, he phoned Bill Haggerty, then managing editor at the *Mirror,* and passed himself off as a "money man" hired by De Lorean himself to make the illegal transactions. A reporter was immediately sent to speak with Flynn; within an hour, £1,500 had been paid to Flynn for the key to a safe-deposit box in Paris which was to contain documents detailing the money transfers. The key actually opened the door to a hotel room in which Flynn had once slept during his travels.

Flynn then phoned De Lorean, posing as a forger hired by the *Mirror* to set him up. For $2,500, Flynn said, he would prove the *Mirror*'s deceit. De Lorean dispatched a couple of heavies to Europe to sit on Flynn until he produced his evidence. They told him that he couldn't leave his hotel room or collect his fee until the evidence was forthcoming. Not daunted in the least, Flynn made a phone call to Haggerty, which De Lorean's men taped.

"Where are the documents?" Haggerty immediately asked. He was getting nervous since he hadn't heard from Flynn for two weeks after the safe-deposit scam.

"I've got them," Flynn said, "and they really look good."

"They look good?" Haggerty replied, falling into the script just as Flynn had planned. Flynn hung up before the true situation was revealed to the heavies and collected his $2,500.

Flynn has conned many European embassies, masquerading as a secret agent or hit man and collecting shopping bags full of money for promises of information or assassination. At a meeting with the Libyan chief of security in Rome, Flynn was invited to meet with Libyan leaders in Tripoli but declined out of fear. The chief of security believed that Flynn was a hit man who worked for the Mafia, and he paid him up front for agreeing to poison some people in London. Flynn was glad to get out of the Libyan embassy with his life.

Flynn has gone to jail only twice. The first time was in Australia during his youth when he served twenty-one weeks for a minor company deception. The second time the charge was more serious, although he spent the majority of his fifteen-month term on remand. (It's not nice to fool the CIA and the FBI, but if you feel you must, it's better to be tried for your crimes in the United Kingdom, as Flynn was, than in the United States.)

The latter case revolved around a Soviet/American double agent named Nicholas Shadrin, a defector to the United States, who disappeared on a rendezvous mission with the KGB in 1975. Flynn read about the disappearance in the *Wall Street Journal* a month afterward and got in touch with Richard Copaken, a Washington lawyer who was acting for Mrs. Shadrin, who was trying to locate her husband. Calling from a telephone booth in Beaulieu, France, Flynn wracked his brain for a name to give Copaken. Noticing an empty Benson & Hedges package on the floor of the booth, he struck on the name *Benson*. Whether this was inspiration or pure coincidence, his choice of monicker paid off. The man who debriefed Shadrin in Moscow was named Benson. Copaken knew this, but no outsider could have known; the information was in a secret file in Washington, D.C. Copaken was immediately convinced that Flynn had the real story on Shadrin. (Copaken, in fact, was never entirely disabused of this belief. As he testified during Flynn's trial, the chances that an outsider could come up with some of the information "Benson" divulged from that telephone booth were roughly equivalent to getting the identical number on a roulette wheel ten times in a row. But then, Flynn was often a lucky gambler.)

The FBI and the CIA began meeting Flynn in London,

flying him around and handing him money, four or five hundred dollars at a time. Over a two-year period, Copaken paid Flynn $3,500 for false leads.

Shadrin was never located, but Copaken continued to insist that Flynn had access to secret files and was a top CIA dis-information man. (Alan Trusman's film script, *The Thomas Crown Affair*, was based in part on Flynn's involvement in the Shadrin case.)

Flynn admits that he is a crook, but apparently remorse doesn't keep him awake at night. He believes that politicians, banks, finance companies, and business institutions are filled with con men, although they may operate within the letter of the law.

"They honestly believe they are honest. I know I'm a crook. Whatever way you flower it up, I'm a crook. But I don't pretend to myself I'm anything else," he says.

THE TERRIBLE TURK

Not all impersonators try to pass as human beings. The Terrible Turk, the nineteenth-century forerunner to *Star Wars'* celebrities R2D2 and C3PO, was billed as a wonderful chess-playing robot. For many years the Turk drew large audiences, amazing the crowds with his mechanical brain. Whirring and whizzing, the funny looking contraption took on anyone who wanted to challenge him, and earned his "inventor," Johan Maelzel, a small fortune in admissions. The hoax finally ended when it was discovered that the machine contained a chess-playing dwarf, who unfortunately remains anonymous.

THE WILD WEST: BUNCO BUCKEROOS

The Old Frontier

Philip Arnold and John Slack, posing as trail-weary prospectors, walked into the Bank of California in San Francisco one hot summer day in 1872. Handing a teller a small sack, they asked him to guard it for them while they paid a little visit to the saloon. The teller agreed. After the prospectors had left, he looked inside the sack, expecting to see a modest amount of gold dust. When instead he found a fortune in uncut diamonds, he rushed to tell his employer, the California wheeler-dealer William Ralston.

Ralston's curiosity was whetted, and so was his avarice. He spent days searching for Arnold and Slack, finally locating them in a bar. After being badgered, wheedled, and bribed by Ralston, they reluctantly admitted the source of the gems. While prospecting in Wyoming, they had come across a diamond field. They did not yet own title to the mineral rights on the land, however, and so did not want anyone else to know its whereabouts. Ralston was able to convince them to take a small party to view the area on the condition that the visitors would be blindfolded after disembarking from the train.

David Colton, Ralston's mining engineer, was speedily dispatched to the field. In company with the prospectors, he traveled to Rawlings, Wyoming, by train. Then he was blindfolded and led a fair distance through rough terrain to the secret location. Colton was astonished. Anthills shimmered like mirages with diamond dust, and great rubies and diamonds littered the ground. Collecting a fistful of stones, he jubilantly returned to San Francisco to give Ralston the good news.

Ralston was delighted with this chance to make what he considered to be a surefire investment. He paid Slack and Arnold $50,000 and put aside $300,000 for their use. He assured them that another $350,000 would be theirs once mining began to produce more revenue. Encouraged by Ralston, other wealthy investors began to pour money into the project, among them Baron Anthony de Rothschild, editor Horace Greeley, General George B. McClellan, and jewelry magnate Charles Lewis Tiffany.

After another inspection party had visited the area, confirming previous reports of vast potential wealth for investors, Ralston began to feel that perhaps the prospectors did not entirely deserve their good fortune. After all, he, Ralston, was backing the enterprise with his own money. Slack and Arnold had done nothing but stumble across a diamond field. Why shouldn't he be the owner of the new mine instead of them? The notion grew on Ralston, and he began to bully the poor prospectors into giving up their rights in the mine. When they resisted his offer of $700,000 for their share, he threatened them with complicated legalities in an attempt to confuse and intimidate them into complicity. Slack and Arnold made a great pretense of trying to hold their own against the robber baron Ralston, but in the end gave in to his demands. Who were they, they intimated, to fight a man of his business acumen and means? Taking the money, they quietly set off for parts unknown.

Right about this time, an expert geologist decided to visit the proposed mine site to check it out for himself. The diamond field was a public sensation, but he was not swept up in the general excitement; he thought that it smelled like a ruse. So E. W. Emmonds traveled to Rawlings and searched the surrounding rangeland.

Emmonds was not long in discovering that the site was near the train station. Arnold and Slack must have led their blindfolded inspection parties around in circles. Furthermore, the gems that still lay on the topsoil had been worked on with lapidary tools, and the anthills were manmade.

When word was wired back to San Francisco, it spread across the entire country within hours. Those who had put up money to finance the project, notably Ralston, did not appear to be particularly amused by the news that the field had been salted with gems, but the public loved it. Ralston's diamond mine changed overnight from an object of envy and greed to a common laughingstock.

It soon came out that Arnold and Slack had planned the scam, spending $350,000 on gems in Europe, then returning to the United States to see who they could fleece. Crime did pay for these two, who were for a time public heroes. They were never prosecuted.

The New Frontier

> *Hold on by letting go, increase by diminishing, and multiply by dividing. These are the principles that have brought me success.*
>
> Billie Sol Estes

> *The sad part of it is that he could have been an honest millionaire instead of a broke crook.*
>
> Bank president, Pecos, Texas

President John F. Kennedy's administration found itself profoundly embarrassed when the scams of West Texas con man Billie Sol Estes came to light. His clever system of using U.S. Department of Agriculture subsidies to help finance his farmland empire was initiated back in Dwight D. Eisenhower's time, but this was little justification for its continuance under Kennedy. Several officials were fired or resigned after it became known that they had accepted expensive suits from Neiman Marcus, paid for in cash by Billie Sol. The implication was that Estes was paying for favors. The public was scandalized that farm subsidies for which they paid so dearly in tax dollars were being spent to amass Billie Sol Estes' fortune rather than to help marginal farmers survive from one year to the next, which was what the funds were to be targeted for. Yet, for all his finagling and courting of favor in high places, Billie Sol was deeply in debt when the scandal broke.

Billie Sol Estes was thirty-seven when first indicted. An

unlikely looking con man, he stood five feet, ten inches tall and weighed in at a pudgy two hundred pounds. With his thick glasses and countrified speech, he may not have appeared exactly impressive. Yet he had made himself the most prominent citizen in Pecos, Texas, and what is more, the world's largest distributor of anhydrous ammonia, a liquid fertilizer that transformed the arid prairies of West Texas into rich cotton land. He also sold insecticides and plows, owned a newspaper, and had formerly owned a funeral home. He entertained important Texas and Washington, D.C., Democrats at his mansion in Pecos. His barbeque was a sight to behold: three steers could be cooked in the pit at the same time. Guests could play tennis on concrete courts or swim in his outdoor pool. There was no drinking of alcoholic beverages, though, and mixed swimming was not allowed, except for married couples.

Billie Sol is quoted as having anxiously asked a friend whether he thought that a fifty-two-foot living room might be "too big." The Estes family filled theirs with expensive furniture, a waterfall, banks of frangipani, and a large cage containing a spider monkey. In the driveway by the green-dyed lawn, Cadillacs from Billie Sol's fleet pulled up and sped away, bearing family members, politicos, and members of the Estes Enterprises girls' softball team. Estes also owned several planes.

An active lay minister in the Pecos Church of Christ, Billie Sol neither drank nor smoked. When his children were in junior high school, he hosted extravagant parties on sock-hop nights to lure the local teens away from the sinful influence of dancing. He was not averse to flashy clothes, but as the years passed his taste grew more conservative, and flamboyant styles were discarded in favor of expensive suits and custom alligator shoes. Despite all the money he made and the polish he acquired, some people in Pecos remained unimpressed, claiming that Estes still talked like a bumpkin.

Billie Sol grew up on a prairie farm in Texas, the son of poor, hardworking parents. The Estes had six children of their own, and had adopted four; it was not easy to make ends meet with ten kids to feed. Billie Sol's mother sold home-churned butter to help out the family finances. Although poor, the Estes had a reputation for honesty.

"We've never had any trouble with this family," Billie Sol's father later said in defense of his son. "Why, I've never even gotten a parking ticket in my whole life."

In describing Billie Sol as a boy of twelve, his father told the following story: "I was plowing behind a team of horses and he came out there to talk to me. I remember he was barefoot. He said he'd been thinking about a tractor and said he thought he could get one in trade for a barn of oats we had. I told him to go ahead and try. He went off and came back with a tractor."

In his desire to make money, Billie Sol often neglected his studies and barely managed to graduate from high school. He prospered at farming, and was later named by the U.S. Junior Chamber of Commerce as one of the nation's ten outstanding young men of 1953. As young Billie Sol was oft heard to remark, "I know I can get rich in fifteen years, but I want to do it in two."

With this goal in mind, he bought up some surplus barracks near the Air Force base near Blythesdale, Arkansas, and had them chain-sawed into sections to be sold as one-family dwellings. These buildings were nothing but shacks, but there was a desperate need for housing around the base, and Billie Sol was able to sell them all at inflated prices.

Although Estes publicly supported minority groups and entertained blacks and Chicanos at his parties (such socializing was rare in Pecos in those days), he was not above using them. For example, in selling his converted barracks, he had persuaded the trustees of Nashville Christian Institute, a Negro school sponsored by the Church of Christ, to pay him

$100,000 of their endowment funds in return for mortgages on the shacks.

Another favorite quote of Billie Sol's was: "If you get into anybody far enough, you've got yourself a partner." In other words, when you owe someone enough money, he acquires a personal interest in your survival and prosperity. He put this theory to work when he became indebted to the Commercial Solvents Chemical Company in New York. He was buying and distributing anhydrous ammonia, a fertilizer necessary to Texas cotton farming. Because the company wanted to see Billie Sol's debt repaid, its management helped him get into the lucrative grain storage business, by which means he could get government money for warehousing surplus grain. The agreement was that he could then continue distributing anhydrous ammonia, which would be supplied to him by Commercial Solvents as he paid off his debts.

The government grain storage program was instituted when postwar agricultural abundance, by the law of supply and demand, began to threaten the farmers' ability to make a buck. It worked basically as follows: In order to keep food prices up by preventing a glut on the market, the government gave a farmer a price-support loan on his crop and then stored it as collateral in a silo or warehouse. The farmer had the choice of keeping the loan and letting the government keep his crop, or selling his crop at a better price and paying the government back the loan. In either case, the certified warehouser was paid a fee at so much a bushel by the Department of Agriculture. If he could buy enough silos and keep them filled, he could get rich.

Using grain-storage money to finance his purchases of anhydrous ammonia, Estes was doing well, but not as well as he had hoped. Other distributors were also selling the fertilizer, thereby cramping his style. Estes proceeded to lower his prices so much so that he drove his competitors out of business. Then, professing to temper the rod with mercy, he bought up their assets cheap. (To break even, the fertilizer had to be sold for $100 a ton; Billie Sol sold it at from $60 to $20 a ton.) "If you shatter an industry," Billie Sol sometimes remarked, "you can pick up all the pieces for yourself." He lost money on this scheme, however, and was later hit with an anti-trust suit.

Another scam, and one which paid off better, at least in the short term, was Billie Sol's anhydrous ammonia storage tank leasing. The fertilizer had to be stored in a certain type of tank. Billie drew up contracts for tank purchase and persuaded farmers to sign them. They were told that, after they bought the tanks, Billie Sol would lease them back at a rate identical to their mortgage payment. As an added inducement, he would pay them each 10 percent of the annual mortgage rate up front. It sounded good to the farmers; Billie Sol sold 32,000 tanks at $10,000 each. Then he turned around and sold the mortgages as collateral to borrow $22 million from commercial finance companies in big cities up north. In order to give the finance companies a false sense of security in the farmers' ability to pay off their mortgages, Estes had secretaries type up phony financial statements on five different typewriters.

Billie Sol was later sued by a farmer for selling him a fertilizer tank he never set his eyes on. This could not have been helped, however, since the tank in question had in fact never existed. As it turned out, most of the mortgaged tanks did not exist, except on paper.

Billie Sol found cotton growing extremely profitable. The only problem he had was that he could not grow enough. In exchange for its generous price supports of cotton, the U.S. government strictly regulated the number of acres a farmer could devote to this crop. A cotton-acreage allotment, determining how much of the land could be devoted to cotton, was attached to a parcel of land. There was no way to transfer that allotment to another piece of land, *except* in cases where eminent domain pertained. Eminent domain refers to the forced sale of land by an individual to the local, state, or federal government. (An example would be the sale of land to the government so that a highway could be built.) If cotton land fell into eminent domain, the farmer would have three years to transfer his cotton allotment to another piece of property.

Estes persuaded Texas, Oklahoma, Georgia, and Alabama farmers who had lost land to eminent domain to buy Texas farmland from him, transfer their allotments to the new land, and then lease him the land and the allotment rights. He would pay a yearly lease amount of $50 an acre. The contract would indicate that the farmer was to pay for the land he bought from Billie Sol in four equal installments. It stipulated that, if he defaulted on the first payment, the land, along with the cotton allotment, would revert to Billie Sol. Billie Sol paid his lease for the first year, at $50 an acre, in advance, with the verbal understanding between himself and the farmer that the farmer would default on the first payment. In this way Billie Sol Estes bought 3,000 acres of cotton allotments in two years.

Billie Sol's battling spirit proved to be his downfall. Running for the Pecos school board on the No Dancing, Segregated Drinking Fountain ticket (*segregated* here meaning separate fountains for boys and girls), he became infuriated with the *Pecos Independent and Enterprise*, the local paper, for campaigning against him. His mood did not improve any after he lost the election. Out to get the *Independent*, he tried to organize a boycott by wives of farmers who owed him money. When this didn't work, he started a rival newspaper and tried to drive the *Independent* out of business by offering advertising space at ridiculously low rates. Those businesses that continued to advertise in the *Independent* were threatened by Estes. In retaliation, the *Independent* researched and printed the first exposure of his storage-tank fraud. The story was picked up by larger papers, and finance investigators, panicky at the thought that the documents they were holding as collateral were not worth the paper they were printed on, came rushing to Pecos from all over the country.

In 1962 Billie Sol Estes was indicted by a federal grand jury for committing fifty-seven acts of fraud. His assets were estimated at $20 million. By his own assessment, his debts were $32 million; the official estimate was closer to $52 million.

Estes pleaded the Fifth, appealed, and generally fought both charges and convictions as stubbornly as anyone could have expected, although his demeanor was anything but belligerent. Polite, subdued, and pious, he surprised a judge who had just handed down his first conviction by saying, "Thank you." He told the press that he did not believe that he would go to jail.

Notwithstanding his efforts to resist incarceration, Estes went to Leavenworth prison in 1965. He was paroled in 1971, under strict orders not to discuss his case with anyone or to engage in self-employment or any promotional activity. Despite his bankruptcy, he was allowed to keep his home, a Cadillac, and other personal assets, and apparently settled down to a quiet home life and the managership of his brother's pig farm outside Abilene. According to an Abilene reporter, however, "Those hogs don't see him very often."

Two deaths, apparently associated with the Billie Sol Estes scandal, have never been explained to everyone's satisfaction. In 1962, after Estes' grain-storage schemes were made public, Henry M. Marshall, a Department of Agriculture agent in charge of cotton allotments in Texas, was found dead in a pasture. He had been shot five times in the abdomen with his own .22 caliber bolt-action rifle. The local sheriff ruled suicide.

Also in 1962, an accountant who had kept books on the

sales of anhydrous ammonia tanks to farmers was found dead in his car. A rubber hose had been run from the exhaust pipe into the interior of the closed car, but an autopsy revealed no carbon monoxide in the man's lungs. Local authorities found the cause of death to be a heart attack.

UNCLE SAM THE FLIMFLAM MAN: GOVERNMENT STINGS

Federal agents, sometimes in cooperation with state and local law-enforcement officials, have been officially carrying out sting operations since 1976. Figuring that two could play at confidence games, government bunco arists have led criminals to wonder who you can trust these days.

The first such operation was set up in California, where seven warehouses for receiving stolen goods were set up. Agents then hit the streets, where they mingled with the underworld, and bought up all of the stolen loot they could get their hands on. Then they threw a warehouse party to celebrate their good fortune, and arrested their illegal suppliers. Millions of dollars' worth of stolen property was recovered, and more than two hundred arrests made in the Los Angeles area.

In Flint, Michigan, federal agents set up a phony fencer, who passed in the criminal world as Mr. Lucky. Heavily disguised, he worked for months at fitting into his new role. After taking in about one million in hot merchandise, he died—or so word had it. At his funeral, sixty crooks were arrested. Mr. Lucky, in reality Walter Ryerson, a Treasury Department investigator, attended his own funeral. He had also taped his transactions.

A government sting operation in New York City entailed a series of scams designed to lure felons of various persuasions out of hiding. The program, the seventh coordinated effort between U.S. Marshals and other federal, state, and local police agencies along the East Coast, led to the capture of 3,309 fugitives. Half of those apprehended on federal warrants were back on the streets after posting bail, but the operation was still judged a success by the U.S. Marshals Service.

Uncle Sam's scams were quite imaginative, and, like many cons, often seemed too simple to work. Some felons were brought out of hiding by disguised agents who infiltrated the neighborhoods where the lawbreakers were believed to be hiding. The agents passed the word around that a large package with no return address was waiting at the post office for a particular suspect. When the suspect got wind of the news, his curiosity often proved stronger than his common sense, and he went in to identify himself and claim his package. Then the police moved in to nab him. One arrestee was lured out of hiding with a phony call from a radio station telling him that he had won a free breakfast with Boy George. When he happily climbed into the limousine dispatched to pick him up, police snapped on the handcuffs.

ABSCAM

Truth is important. I learned from an old con man, never lie when you don't have to lie. . . . You have to try to put yourself into the position and then believe it so much that you feel that you're tellin' the truth. I believe that before you sell a deal, you have to live the deal. . . . Now as to hope. That's another important thing. A guy is in a jam and he comes to me for money. Under my breath I might say "f——— you," but I don't say that. Because when a guy is in a jam and lookin' for money it's my philosophy to give hope. Everybody has to have hope. That's why most people don't turn us into the cops. They keep hopin' we're for real.

Melvin Weinberg, government-hired con artist
Robert W. Greene, *The Sting Man: Inside Abscam*

The most famous government sting operation to date is ABSCAM. When the two-year investigation was over, the public was shocked to learn that Congressmen and other elected officials had taken bribes and given favors to obvious crooks in order to line their own pockets. The undercover operation was sponsored by the FBI in connection with the Justice Department, but its real star was a short, balding con artist named Melvin Weinberg.

At the time of his first arrest, Weinberg had been an extremely successful con man, some say the best in the business, for thirty-five years. U.S. and overseas financial scams had netted him millions of dollars. He had a fine home, a loyal wife and family, and a beautiful mistress (known as Lady Diane), whose obvious class helped him sway many a mark. Weinberg's Bronx accent, flavored with underworld slang, and gangsterish taste in clothes, cars, and diamond pinky rings were offset by Lady Diane's aristocratic looks and manners. While she was, according to Weinberg, an unwitting accomplice in his dishonest dealings, the two made an all-but-unbeatable pair.

In 1977, after his arrest on charges of fraud, Weinberg had nearly everything going for him and was sure that he could beat the rap. What, then, induced him to go to work for the FBI? Not the salary, which at $1,000 a month was peanuts to a businessman of Weinberg's caliber. Not the company—he considered his associates in the program to be a bunch of boy scouts, hopelessly inept at pulling off a sting. Not the funding, which was pitifully low and didn't allow for the expensive props essential to a big-time con. Not idealism, either: Weinberg figured that politicians were all a bunch of crooks. No, Weinberg's motivation in pleading guilty to fraud and accepting the FBI's offer of a steady job hinged around Lady Diane. The authorities had him by the short hairs. Either he bargained with them or they brought charges against his mistress. As Weinberg said, you can only be so much of a heel in this life.

Weinberg was the one who dreamed up the concept of disguising an agent as an Arabian sheikh in order to entice white-collar criminals into the FBI trap. He knew that everyone thought all Arabs were rich, and correctly assumed that the promise of limitless oil money would trigger a Pavlovian reaction among prospective marks. ABSCAM stands for *Abdul Scam.* Weinberg and FBI agents acted as representatives of two Arab sheikhs, Kambir Abdul Rahman and Yassir Habib. The Arabs, of course, were disguised agents.

In the beginning, there was a lot of trouble with costuming, speech, and inadvertent nervous giggling. The first sheikh, Abdul, and a female agent had to duck into a bedroom during the early days of the operation to avoid bursting into laughter. Weinberg covered up for them by explaining to a surprised client that Abdul went crazy around women when he was out of the restrictive atmosphere of his native land; he and his secretary were always running off to the bedroom. The client believed him. After that misadventure, Tony Amoroso was ushered into the picture as Sheikh Yassir Habib, replacing Abdul. Weinberg and Amoroso became friends and worked well together.

ABSCAM might never have been responsible for the conviction of so many high-ranking officials had it not been for the tapes that documented every transaction. Taping everything was Weinberg's idea, too. He initiated this procedure in order to save his own neck in case the FBI accused him of duplicity or tried to put blame on him for imaginary shortcomings. He wanted everything that transpired in ABSCAM to be a matter of record.

The bogus sheikh's representatives explained to the hoodlums, con men, and—later—mobsters, mayors, and Congressmen, that Abdul and Yassir wanted to move to the United States. First, however, they had to get their money out of Saudi Arabia, and this was allowable only by certain specialized methods.

Weinberg and the agents intimated that the sheikhs would gladly pay huge sums of money in return for "favors." As the sting operation progressed, the FBI learned a great deal about corruption in the American political process. It came out that the Mob, working with and through local officials, controlled casino gambling in Vegas and Atlantic City. The fact that many elected officials were easily persuaded to take bribes was also established. Philadelphia Congressman Michael J. Myers, accepting a small fortune from Tony Amoroso, told him that he was going about things the right way. "I'm gonna tell you something simple and short. Money talks in this business and bullshit walks. And it works the same way down in Washington." At one point Angelo J. Erichetti, mayor of Camden, New Jersey, brought in a ringer and tried to con Weinberg with a phony deal. Weinberg didn't go for it.

All of this was on video tape; otherwise it might have been difficult for jurors to swallow. All meetings in which payoffs were made could be played and replayed on courtroom video screens. Rooms where the transactions took place had been bugged with cameras hidden in television sets, light fixtures, and walls. Special lenses enabled scenes to be taped through tiny holes.

Many of the ABSCAM cons bore the stamp of Weinberg's divine—or infernal—inspiration. To nab some art thieves, he convinced the suspects to meet with him at night at a remote county airport in New York State. There, under the cover of darkness, Weinberg, his "art expert," and the pilot—both FBI agents—were to meet with the thieves. Enroute to the rendezvous, Weinberg carried a suitcase purported to contain $750,000 in bills, but actually containing torn-up pages from a telephone book. (Life sometimes imitates art; Weinberg's plot was inspired by a television movie.) It worked at any rate, and agents collected enough evidence to nail the thieves and seize the stolen art treasure.

It was also Weinberg's idea to have a party thrown by Yassir for Mayor Erichetti aboard a yacht moored at Fort Lauderdale's Pier 66. A multitude of politicians and criminals of every calling was invited to attend. Weinberg was not happy with the arrangements; for one thing, the whole operation had been severely underbudgeted. How were they supposed to snow the assembled guests with a low-rent bash? He was somehow able to get the yacht overhauled and fancied up, charm some prominent citizens into providing appropriate food and drink, and costume himself and the other agents for the occasion, but only just in the nick of time. And the FBI adamantly refused to spring for prostitutes, despite Weinberg's heartfelt protests that the guests would expect some entertainment. Yassir made a short appearance, presenting the guest of honor with a "tribal ceremonial sword" supposedly passed down in his family for generations. The heirloom sword was in actuality a cheap imitation picked up in a flea market for about three dollars. Mayor Erichetti was overcome with emotion. Later, thinking back on all of the schemes in rampant play aboard the yacht, Weinberg referred to the party as "the Con Boat."

ABSCAM was to result in the conviction of many white-collar crooks, including some high-up officials. Among those convicted of accepting bribes were Michael J. Myers; Angelo J. Erichetti; Representative Raymond F. Lederer of Pennsylvania; Representative Frank Thompson, Jr., of New Jersey; Representative John M. Murphy of New York; Representative John W. Jenrette of South Dakota; and Representative Richard Kelly of Florida. Both Jenrette and Myers attempted to explain away their bad behavior by explaining that they accepted bribes because they were drunk at the time, but jurors refused to be swayed by such alibis.

And whatever happened to Mel Weinberg, master con man, after the ABSCAM trials were finished? Well, he went straight, boys and girls. How could he ever hope to keep a low profile after all that publicity? By his own admission, he would never be able to pull it off.

Ronald Rewald: CIA Spy or Civilian Con Man?

Bishop, Baldwin, Rewald, Dillingham & Wong, a Hawaii-based investmant company, went bankrupt in July 1983, leaving four hundred investors out approximately $20.4 million. Celebrities, retired military men of high rank, prominent businessmen, and the former CIA representative in Honolulu and his successor were among the victims of this elaborately advertised Ponzi scam. When a Honolulu news program broadcast the findings of investigators—that Ronald Rewald, founder of the investment company, was neither as respectable nor as successful a businessman as he had pretended to be—Rewald checked into a hotel room and slit his wrists. The assistant manager found him late the next afternoon lying in a pool of blood. He had cut deeply into his wrists and forearms, but had not managed his suicide any better than he had managed Bishop, Baldwin, Rewald, Dillingham, & Wong.

After his recovery, Rewald made a statement that was at first disregarded as just one more bunco excuse: He claimed that he was a covert agent for the CIA and that his company had been a CIA front. As we shall see, Rewald had lied about almost everything else concerning his business and personal life. This cloak-and-dagger intrigue seemed to be just one more false story among many. But several months later, nobody could be sure where the lies ended and the truth began.

It is not surprising that Rewald was able to dupe so many sophisticated and well-educated investors when one considers that the Securities and Exchange Commission (SEC), which regulates investment and other securities operations, and the IRS both lent their implicit approval to his enterprise.

Rewald and his partner, Sunlin Wong, named their company after themselves and several of the old Hawaiian *Kamaaina* families, nineteenth-century settlers who amassed great wealth in the islands, and who are still highly respected in Hawaii today. The names lent credibility to the company, drawing attention away from its true, fly-by-night nature. It didn't hurt, either, that Bishop, Baldwin was often advertised as having been in operation for forty years ("since territorial days"), and having served four administrations. Investors were told that Bishop, Baldwin offices were located in cities from Tahiti to London.

The firm's investors were insured for up to $150,000 by the Federal Deposit Insurance Corporation (FDIC), said Rewald, who also stated that the accounts were tax-deferred.

In truth, no *Kamaaina* families had anything to do with the firm; the SEC had approved Rewald's license without checking his background (which is not at all unusual for this commission); and the IRS had, for reasons unknown, agreed to defer an investigation that had begun in 1982. The company had been in operation for about five years at the time of its collapse, rather than forty; the offices stretching from Tahiti to London were nothing more than mail drops; and the FDIC did not insure investments made in Bishop, Baldwin. (The federal government covers only bank accounts, and not for more than $100,000 in any one account.)

Rewald's downfall must have come as a surprise to those who had known him only since his arrival in Hawaii. He dressed well, lived extravagantly, and maintained an air of solid respectability. His children were chauffeured to and from classes in a limousine. He and his family lived in a shorefront mansion bought in 1980 for $950,000. He also owned a couple of Hawaiian ranches, a fleet of classic cars, and a string of polo ponies. He bought the failing Hawaii Polo Club, shored it up with his own funds, and wrote up a dress code to give the place some additional class. There he made new business contacts and entertained investors in style. Four bodyguards watched over his home and family.

According to an affadavit by Rewald which has since been suppressed by the CIA, he was hired by the CIA during the 1960s to spy on radical groups at the University of Wisconsin at Madison, earning $120 a week in cash for nine months' undercover work. The dean who Rewald says referred him to the CIA has stated that he has no recollection of the matter. Rewald's diploma from Marquette University, displayed in his Bishop, Baldwin office has been determined to be a forgery; he never graduated from an institution of higher education. Neither did he play football with the semipro Wisconsin Raiders, as he was wont to boast to those who would listen.

He did own the College Athletic Supply Company in Milwaukee, where he engaged in double-entry bookkeeping, began business meetings with prayers, and spent many afternoons engaging in extramarital flings with different women, one of whom was reputed by a former associate to have been a CIA secretary. On his way back to the College Athletic Supply office, he routinely stopped at the Marquette University chapel for confession. When his business began to go downhill, Rewald started selling franchises.

Because Rewald did not keep the franchise stores stocked as he had contracted to do, the franchisees also began to go under. The state of Wisconsin stepped in and charged Rewald for failure to register with the state and for making untrue and misleading statements to franchisees. He pleaded guilty to a misdemeanor. In 1975 both College Athletic Supply and Rewald went bankrupt.

Soon afterward Rewald applied for, and received, SEC registration. He was careful to omit any reference to his previous conviction, and passed himself off as a Marquette graduate. In 1977 the Rewald family moved to Hawaii with borrowed funds and set up the investment company that was to be named Bishop, Baldwin, Rewald, Dillingham & Wong.

But what about the CIA? Court documents reveal that Rewald has testified that the CIA told him to set up Bishop, Baldwin as a front for covert arms sales to Taiwan and as a base for industrial spying operations on Japan. CIA officials admit alternately to no involvement with Bishop, Baldwin and slight involvement. One official allowed that the firm provided some cover for agents; others have stated it was used only as a mail drop. Court records show that the CIA paid Bishop, Baldwin $2,700 for phone bills. Rewald also maintains that the mysterious halt in the IRS investigation of Bishop, Baldwin was prompted by CIA contacts. Several investors have filed claims against the CIA on the grounds that the agency should not have allowed investors to be bilked. CIA officials deny any responsibility or involvement in investors' complaints.

The strangest part of the Bishop, Baldwin incident is the story of Scott Barnes, which he told on ABC's "World News Tonight." Barnes said that he had been hired by the CIA to take a prison guard job at the institution where Rewald was incarcerated for five and a half months after his arrest, in order to keep an eye on him. Barnes also claims that CIA officials told him, "We gotta take him (Rewald) out."

The CIA angrily refuted the story. "As ABC knows," the denial read, "the CIA, along with the rest of the U.S. government, is prohibited by law from engaging in, or contemplating, assassination." The Agency demanded a retraction of the story by ABC.

At first, the network refused and declared it would stand by its story. Later, though, it amended its version by stating over the air: "Charges cannot be substantiated, and we have no reason to doubt the CIA's denial." This was not enough, though, for the Agency.

Because the Supreme Court has indicated that federal

agencies cannot sue news organizations for libel, the CIA took the unprecedented step of appealing to the Federal Communications Commission (FCC), requesting that ABC be forced to retract "all false allegations." Otherwise, the CIA suggested, the FCC should consider not renewing the contracts of ABC-owned stations. In January 1985, the CIA's requests were officially denied.

And so the matter stands. Legal procedures against Rewald have not at this writing yet ground to a halt. At the Agency's request, a U.S. district court judge in Hawaii has sealed all documents regarding Rewald and Bishop, Baldwin on the grounds of national security.

What was the CIA's involvement in Bishop, Baldwin, Rewald, Dillingham & Wong? Chances are we will never know the whole story.

4.

Classic Cons

And there is no new thing under the sun.
Ecclesiastes 1.10

Possibilities for cons are as endless as the ingenuity of con artists. With every technological advance or shift in public opinion, games come popping up like mushrooms after a summer rain. The advent of air travel and the widespread use of the telephone and computer, for example, paved the way for airport terminal hustles, fraudulent boiler-room operations, and investment scams (which owe their credibility to phony but impressive-looking computer printouts). Although these cons are modern, each is rooted in an old tradition. Prolific as the con artist is in churning out crimes to fit the times, he still uses principles and frameworks laid down by the old classics, some of which have been in successful operation for hundreds of years. This is hardly surprising when you think that human nature has not changed over the years and that exploitation of human nature is the con man's bread and butter. Familiarity with the principles and techniques of classic cons will give you an edge in recognizing their countless offshoots, variations, and modifications.

Classic cons are divided into two categories, the *big con* and the *short con*. Both are relatively short-term operations.

It usually takes the con man anywhere from one day to several weeks to find, set up, and bilk his mark. He then drops out of the mark's life, never (he hopes) to be seen or heard from again. In the big con, the mark is *put on the send,* or sent out to get a large sum of money at some point during the game, whereas in the short con he is taken only for the amount he has on his person. Sometimes a con man will combine the two and put the mark on the send in what is otherwise essentially a short con.

THE BIG CON

The big con is living theater: Two or more con men work together, using scripting, acting, and often stage sets, props, and costume, to stage a performance. No detail is neglected in the creation of this "separate reality," although the cost may run into thousands of dollars. When the mark is ushered into the artificial world made solely for his benefit, he is the only person there who doesn't know the score. He seldom suspects that he is the only one playing it straight in an elaborate production designed for the express purpose of defrauding him. Were the thought to occur to him, he would probably dismiss it as paranoia. Considering the talent, work, and expense that con artists put into these games, it's no wonder that so many otherwise sharp businessmen have fallen for them over the years.

Traditionally, ten steps are followed in performing any big con operation.

1) *Locating a suitable mark,* someone with enough available money to make the game worthwhile.
2) *Playing the con,* or gaining the confidence of the mark by whatever means of persuasion the con man deems appropriate.
3) *Roping the mark* means guiding the mark to the *insideman,* another con man, who presides over the phony

establishment set up for the purpose of separating the mark from his money. These first three steps are performed by the *outsideman,* or *roper.* The latter term calls to mind a cowboy, whose job it is to round up cattle and drive them in to slaughter, and for good reason.

4) *Telling the tale.* The insideman explains to the mark how he can make a quick and dirty fortune. This con role requires both sales and acting ability, as well as a flair for amateur psychology, for the insideman must guide and control the mark as the game progresses.

5) *Delivering the convincer.* This phrase refers to the money the mark is initially allowed to make, supposedly by means of the dishonest method introduced to him by the insideman. The convincer acts as an appetizer, sharpening the mark's hunger for greater gains and convincing him that such gains are possible. It also implicates the mark; he feels that, as he has now profited by dishonest dealings, he might as well go all the way (better to be hung for a sheep than a lamb).

6) *Calculating the breakdown.* The insideman figures out how much money the mark is good for.

7) *Putting the mark on the send.* The insideman now encourages the mark to take his money out of the bank, sell his business, beg, borrow, steal, or use any other means at his disposal to procure a large sum of money. Because of the convincer, the mark now believes that this money will be multiplied many times over.

8) *Putting the touch on.* The mark is taken for everything he has invested in the game. (Also called *the sting* or *the score.)*

9) *Blowing off the mark.* Getting rid of the mark. If the blow-off is skillfully executed, the victim will never realize that he has been conned.

One dramatic and effective blow-off is the old *cackle bladder* routine. In a carefully staged performance, a "gunman," who may be playing the role of a policeman, irate loser, or mobster, shoots and apparently kills one or more people involved in the venture. It is, of course, all illusion. Blank cartridges are used, and, for the sake of realism, the man who is to be shot carries a small, blood-filled balloon in his mouth so that he can ooze convincingly on cue. (The blood of choice has traditionally come from chickens, and hence the name *cackle bladder.)* The murder victim may manage to lurch over and spew blood on the mark's clothes, while the murderer places the gun in the mark's hand before expeditiously leaving the scene of the crime. Covered in gore, holding the still-warm murder weapon, and watching the place empty out like a schoolroom when the bell rings, the mark will feel a queasy combination of bewilderment, guilt, and fear. He vacates the premises as quickly as possible and thereafter does his best to hide all traces of his involvement with his former "business associates." He is unlikely to go to the police, first because he does not even know that he has been the victim of a con game, and second, because he believes that he is guilty of shady dealings himself. His third reason for avoiding the law is fear of implication in the murder that he thinks he has witnessed.

10) *Putting in the fix.* This step may be performed at any stage of the game. It may refer to bribery of police officials in the area of operation or to convincing the mark, in one way or another, not to go to the authorities.

There are three classic big con games: *the wire, the pay-off,* and *the rag.*

The Wire

The original big con, the wire, dates back to the late 1800s. It was made possible by the invention of the telegraph wire, from which it gets its name. In those days, Western Union used to telegraph horse-race results from eastern and southern tracks to its main office in Chicago. From there, the results were transmitted to horse parlors, where betting was performed, throughout the Windy City. Professional telegraph operators at these parlors translated the messages as they came in from Morse code to spoken English for the benefit of the bettors. Although today no bet is accepted after post time (the moment the horses leave the post), at that time bets were made and taken until the telegrapher at the horse parlor began announcing the official race results.

Naturally, it soon occurred to certain devious individuals that the gap in time between the arrival of race results at the main Western Union office and the announcement of those results at the parlor might somehow be turned to advantage. A telegrapher might, for instance, tap into the main line, getting the race results before the betting ended. Or, when the results arrived at the parlor, the telegrapher could slip a partner the winner's name, withholding the information from the rest of the establishment until after a foolproof bet had been placed. A third alternative entailed collaboration between two telegraphers and a third partner. One telegrapher, a corrupt Western Union employee working in the main office, would send a coded advance message to his confederate in a horse parlor, such as "Dreadnaught is holding the horses up at the post." The horse parlor telegrapher would announce this bit of fallacious news, and this was the third partner's cue to go and place his bet on Dreadnaught. Soon afterward, the main office telegrapher would transmit the horse-race results as if he had just received them. In all of these scams, the bettor was able to profit with little or no risk to himself. The legal and professional risk for the dishonest telegrapher was, however, great.

The creators of the wire game turned the tables on the bettor by staging the preceding scenarios, realizing that more money could be won with less risk to themselves by *pretending* to give secret information than by actually doing so. A con man played the part of the dishonest telegrapher. He allowed his "partner," the mark, to win several small bets as a convincer, put him on the send, and then fleeced him. The mark was blown off by attributing the incorrect placing of his bet to a bookmaker's error. Even if he suspected that he had been cheated, however, he was hardly likely to go to the police and report his part in an illegal activity.

The wire game was refined over the years to include phony Western Union offices and horse parlors, elaborate stage sets capable of fooling any mark, especially one giddy at the prospect of raking in vast amounts of easy money. These phony establishments, called *stores,* or *big stores,* were manned by a *con mob,* a cast of suitably costumed grifters playing the roles of telegraphers, bookmakers, bettors, messenger boys, and others. Confidence men acted as ropers, rounding up prospective marks from all over the city and bringing them into the store to be fleeced.

Joe Weil, better known in some circles as the Yellow Kid, became adept at the wire and made several additional refinements to the game. His method of operation was in fact so complicated that it was a wonder it worked at all. Yet work it did, time after time.

Rather than set up a Western Union store, he used the real thing, hiring another con man with acting talent, Billy Wall, to play the part of a disgruntled telegrapher. Weil was the roper; he took his mark to meet the phony telegrapher at the Western Union office. Wall, appropriately attired for the role, would be approached by Weil to perform the *golden wire* for them. (The golden wire was a system whereby a telegrapher would send coded advance race results from Western Union to a horse parlor, holding back the official announcement long enough to allow the bettor to place his bet. Weil told the mark that it was a sure thing.)

Wall played the part of the hard-to-get telegrapher perfectly, whetting the mark's appetite for the game. Meetings were arranged at the telegrapher's home, a rented house furnished for the occasion, where the mark was introduced to Wall's supposed wife, an actress Weil had hired. Wall would finally relent and agree to go along with the deal, letting the mark think that he had been talked into it.

Entering the horse-parlor store, the mark was the only person playing it straight in a well-rehearsed, authentically staged theatrical production, complete with hired actors, lots of cash changing hands, and a real Western Union wire. The frenzied activity and flowing money, combined with the success of several modest bets, affected the mark like a drug. The send would be easy once the mark experienced this first euphoric rush of greed.

One victim, a man named Weinholt, sold his delicatessen in order to place a bet that he figured was a sure thing. The telegraph wire and the received race results were real. What Weinholt and other victims before and after him did not realize was that the "special advance messages" coming in over the so-called golden wire were merely the official race results, legally transmitted by the main office, and fraudulently read out by the parlor telegrapher to suit the purposes of the wire con. The conspiracy of secret, coded information and delayed announcement of race results in which Weinholt believed himself to be participating was pure sham.

After losing $12,000 (money from the sale of the deli), supposedly because of a "false tip from the main office," the furious Weinholt was cooled by the sight of Billy Wall (actually a wax effigy) in his coffin. The Western Union man,

Weil explained, had obviously fouled up the golden wire as a result of a fatal illness. Now, here he lay dead, as anyone could plainly see. Why not be philosophical about it? After all, you can't argue with The Reaper.

Like some hopped-up Lazarus, the telegrapher died and came back to life over and over again. It was not until a golden-wire victim recognized Billy Wall at the racetrack one day that Yellow Kid Weil decided it was time to hang up the wire and go on to other scams.

For those who would like to see the wire con illustrated, *The Sting*, an excellent movie starring Paul Newman and Robert Redford, is recommended. It is sometimes difficult to envision a complicated con game in progress and equally difficult to imagine how anyone could be taken in by tricks which seem so implausible on paper. *The Sting* delivers a fast-paced and believable account of the way in which the classic big con was performed, elucidating all ten steps, including a cackle-bladder blow-off!

The Payoff

Developed in 1906, the payoff was perfected in 1910 by the addition of the big store (usually a pool hall with betting in the back room) as a stage for the action. It is still played *against the wall*, i.e., without benefit of the big store, in low-budget operations. The payoff is similar to the wire in that the mark is conned into believing that he will receive sure-fire betting tips by dishonest means. In this scam, the inside information allegedly comes from a network that fixes horse races and thus can call the winners in advance. As in other big cons, the mark is usually hooked so that he begs to be let in on the deal and feels himself lucky when the insideman "lets him play."

The mark may be sitting at his favorite bar, minding his own business, when the talk at a nearby table begins to increase in volume and excitement. Gradually, he grows interested and glances over. What to his wondering eyes should appear but cash—large stacks of it—laid out like Scrooge's wildest dream. Now his interest is intense. As one of the men stashes the loot in a briefcase, the mark listens attentively to the continuing conversation. He feels somewhat embarrassed at eavesdropping, never dreaming that the little show has been put on just for him. One of the men at the neighboring table is a roper and the other is a *shill,* or accomplice. They are expert at their work, and so give the mark an opportunity to include himself in their discussion rather than approaching him.

"Excuse me, but I, um, couldn't help but overhear. Were you saying that you won all that in a game that's going on around here? Can anyone get in on it? Listen, could I buy you guys a beer?"

"I'm the one that ought to be buying," the shill says, laughing as if he is awed by the good fortune he has just stumbled upon. He lowers his voice. "All right, I'll tell you about it, but this is between us, OK? You don't look like a cop, but this shouldn't really get around." He looks over at the roper, as if asking if he's making a mistake by talking too much.

The roper starts to complain, then reluctantly indicates his assent by shrugging noncommitally. "Just keep your voice down—and don't go opening that briefcase again. I'll get the beer."

The shill lets on that he won the money that night betting on the horses. His friend introduced him to the people who made it possible and is now trying to calm him down and get him home before he blows it. The mark convinces the two men to take him to the place where the betting is going on.

At the pool hall, the roper introduces the mark to the insideman, who also appears reluctant to admit a stranger to the club. Finally he agrees, explaining that the races are fixed and that the winners' names will be supplied by messenger. The mark is introduced to the bookmaker and shortly afterward given the name of the next winner. The race is already over and the results a matter of record, but the mark does not know this. The acting has all been very convincing, and, more important, he *wants* to believe that his luck has turned and he is finally in on a good thing. Had the roper pitched the deal to him in the bar, the mark would have been suspicious and resisted the offer, despite the stack of bills. As it happened, however, he was the one that begged to be allowed to participate in the action, and this has affected his mindset about the entire operation.

It helps, too, that the tips he gets for the first few races are good. He wins every time, and collects more money than he usually sees in a month. Rather than satisfy him, the money he's won only makes him speculate how much more he could garner were he to place larger bets. The convincer has done its job; now the mark is put on the send by the insideman, who suggests that if he hurries over to the computerized bank teller to withdraw his savings up to the bank's limit, he will still have time to make the last race. The mark needs little encouragement to do so.

Fresh from the bank, the mark is now presented with an old line. "Place it all on Invincible," the insideman whispers. "And get a move on." Naturally, the mark puts his wad on Invincible, but Invincible places and the mark loses everything.

"Place!" the insideman hisses, as if he can't believe the mark's stupidity. "Place!" Don't you know what that means?"

Before the mark can close his mouth, much less gather his wits, a shill elbows through the crowd to inform them that there is going to be a bust—the law is onto the race fixing and heading this way. Somewhere in the distance sirens whine.

The mark's disappointment now gives way to fear, as everyone around him jumps out of the windows and pushes through the doorway three abreast, like rats deserting a sinking ship. The panic is contagious, and the mark takes off, too.

The evening is not a total loss; as he arrives at his own front door, he realizes that he must have just run at least three miles, a new personal record. And he managed to get away before the cops came, too. He wonders how many of the others involved in the fixed betting were able to escape.

Days later, he cruises past the pool hall, but it is boarded up. Too bad, he thinks, the owners must have been arrested. Now he won't get a chance to recoup his loss. He waits at the bar, hoping to see his "friend," the roper. The roper never shows, and the mark grows accustomed to the same old daily routine. It never occurs to him that his big adventure, when he came so close to making out like a bandit, was all a con.

The successful blow-off is not unusual. Con artists frequently tell stories about running into people whom they have fleeced, only to be asked for another chance to play the game. So great is the confidence some of these scammers instill that their victims will hunt them down, not to exact revenge but for the opportunity to try again. While con artists are known to be second only to fishermen in veracity, there is doubtless a grain of truth to the stories.

The Rag

The rag is basically the same as the payoff, but in this game the mark is offered inside information on stocks or other securities instead of racing tips. (A man who is knowledgeable about the horses is more likely to be played for the rag, while someone who is knowledgeable about stocks is more likely to be played for the payoff.)

The mark need not be unsophisticated or totally ignorant of financial matters to be duped by this con, however. Businessmen are the primary targets of con men working the rag. They are frequently approached during the course of a business trip, on board an airplane, or on the subway or commuter bus. It works like this: The mark may be seated between two men who are conducting a conversation about stocks. As time passes, he grows friendly with the two men, who are dressed for success, personable, and obviously extremely sharp professionally. One of the men refers him to a stockbroker in the city the mark will be visiting. This guy is a genius, the man tells him; he can double your investment in a day. He is cautioned to keep quiet, as the deal is not strictly legal.

The store is a plush stockbroker's office, equipped with a mass of constantly ringing phones. These are handy for the insideman, who can be constantly "interrupted" by calls during the course of his conversation with the mark. He will be able to give a great impression of his financial prowess by means of these conversations, thus obviating the need to boast to his new client. The mark thinks that he is observing the broker in action, and this is far more persuasive than any personal account the broker could give. Never mind that the seemingly spontaneous calls have all been carefully prepared and rehearsed. The mark will never know this.

The role of the stockbroker is that of a winner—wealthy and dependable. The mark trusts him because of his obvious success, which he measures in part by the appearance of the office, the dress and manner of the broker, the brisk pace of the daily business, and even the incessant clatter of typewriters and the good looks of the women who sit at them.

The game plan is the same as in the other big cons. The mark receives his convincer, is put on the send for more money, which he may have cabled to him, and then fleeced by means of one ruse or another. The sting typically comes in the guise of an inside tip wrongly interpreted. The law is often used as the heavy for the blow-off; the broker is supposedly forced to abandon a particular scheme because the authorities are on to him and are breaking up the operation.

A Word to the Wise

Illusion is the con man's secret weapon—and a remarkably potent one, because most people accept what they see at face value. In the rag and other investment cons, the big-store office is a masterpiece of deception. The office inspires confidence because its busy atmosphere and lavish appurtenances suggest stability, wealth, and success. The smell of big money is as reassuring to a mark as the aroma of grandma's apple pie, and he seldom questions its authenticity.

Melvin Weinberg, by virtue of his proven skills as a confidence artist, was hired by the feds to bribe politicians for ABSCAM. In his book *The Sting Man*, Robert W. Greene describes Weinberg's business office in the days before the huge government sting operation took up all of Weinberg's time. Color-coordinated carpeting, draperies, and furniture (all of the finest quality), constantly ringing telephones, and a pervasive sense of big deals in the making set a mood highly conducive to duping investors. The office staff, all hustle and bustle in more ways than one, also played its part in the scenario. The women were selected largely on the basis of looks and style. Although they were ignorant of the dishonest nature of the business they conducted, they were a substantial asset to the con. The cost of Weinberg's office was immense, but he recouped his initial outlay within the first month of operation. The illusion was worth every penny.

Not everyone falls for the big store, however. At least one U.S. banker, according to *Fortune* magazine, was experienced enough to see through the facade created by George Tan, perpetrator of a gigantic banking scam in Hong Kong. By citing fictitious backers, Tan was able to borrow millions of dollars from banks to finance a paper empire in real estate. Before his conglomerate crashed, Tan owed much of his transient but stupendous success to fast talk and flash.

"The moment I walked into Tan's office—with marble

statues, a fountain, and Louis XIV furniture—it was too sur-
real to be believed," the unflappable banker said. "He just
impressed me as a used car salesman."

THE SHORT CON

The classic short cons are so numerous that it would be
impossible to describe them all. Some of the more common
short cons, though, are explained below.

Short cons often seem so simple that it is difficult to imagine how anyone could be fooled by them. Oddly enough,
those cons that seem most questionable—the pigeon drop and
the bank examiner, to name two examples—continue to work
generation after generation. As one con man said, "The con
who works the short con has got to believe in it himself, or
he can't pull it off. Some are too smart. They say, 'this'll
never work,' and so it doesn't. You gotta believe in your
con or you won't make anyone else believe it."

Any of these games may be tailored to suit the con man's
taste, circumstances, or relationship with his mark. The game
itself is merely a basic blueprint, which can be modified when
necessary.

Block Hustle

One of the simplest confidence games, the block hustle, is
usually the domain of younger men who have not yet
acquired a high degree of expertise. Con men are competitive
among themselves, and it is an insult for one con to accuse
another of ineptness at any scam outside of a block hustle.

If you have ever spent much time in a big city, you have
probably seen the block hustler or heard his pitch: "Hey!
Wanna buy a di'mond ring?"

The implication is that his wares are stolen and that he is
fencing them for a quick profit. Because he needs to get rid
of his merchandise in a hurry, he is willing to sell it at a fraction of its true cost.

The reality is that the goods he hawks are usually fakes that have been manufactured specifically for this type of sale. The genuine diamond ring is worthless, the good-looking watch has no jewels, the name-brand perfume (frequently Chanel No. 5) is some cheap substitute, resembling its namesake only in color.

Another item which has been hustled on the street for many years is the wind-up barking dog. It does move around when it is wound up. While the prospective customers watch the toy, the hustler barks. Very often, the delighted audience falls for the trick. I know a woman who once brought home one of these amazing barking dogs, wound it up for her husband, and sat back waiting for it to bark.

"What's the matter?" her husband asked, seeing the look of disappointment on her face.

"It isn't barking," she said. "It barked on the street, and the salesman told me it was guaranteed to bark."

"I'm surprised he didn't tell you it could talk, too," her husband said.

Once a person is familiar with the block hustle, he isn't likely to fall for it, but there are enough unwary citizens on the streets to make this con worth a hustler's while. A good block hustler can make up to $150 a day. Of course, by the time his customers realize their mistake, he is nowhere to be found.

Pigeon Drop

The pigeon drop, also known as the wallet drop or envelope drop, is typically used on middle-aged or elderly women deemed likely to have a savings account. Such women, referred to as *moms*, are the favorite prey of many con artists. The pigeon drop can, however, be played on anyone, man or woman.

To illustrate this game, let's say that an elderly woman is window-shopping when she is approached by a younger woman, whom we'll call con woman A. Con woman A makes a little polite conversation about the weather, then asks if the older woman has lived long in the area. If so, could she recommend a good doctor? The young woman is new here, her little boy is sick, and she doesn't know where to go for help. As she talks, she pulls her billfold out of her purse and shows the mom some photographs of her children. While these two are admiring the babies, con woman B, apparently just happening by, exclaims excitedly, "Oh my goodness! Did one of you just drop a wallet?" She holds up a wallet and opens it, revealing that it is stuffed with money.

The other two admit that it does not belong to them, and the trio then stands around trying to decide what to do. At this point in the game, the mom may suggest they call the police. When she makes this suggestion, the con artists are usually history before the mom has time to suit action to the word. The short-con artist has an allergic reaction to such suggestions and reacts in a similar way when the mark decides to consult a spouse, family member, or close friend.

If the mom does not make any suggestions of this nature, the con women come up with one of their own. Con woman B says that she will take the wallet to her lawyer (or supervisor, banker, or some other authoritative individual) to get his opinion. She says that if he thinks it would be all right, she will split the money with the other two women. She then agrees to meet them at a designated time and place.

Con woman A and the mom adjourn for coffee and wait for con woman B to return. Con woman A stays with the mom at all times to make sure that she doesn't get in touch with anyone. Eventually con woman B comes in, all excited, and informs them that her lawyer has outlined the correct legal procedure for handling the found money. He will place it in a bank deposit box and, as no identification was discovered in the wallet, he will put an advertisement in the personals column of the local paper. If after a certain number of days, no claimant can prove ownership of the money, the three women can divide it equally among themselves. There is only one catch, she says, but one that should cause no trouble. As a sign of good faith, each of the three must withdraw matching sums from the bank—in this case, $1,000—and place their money in the safe-deposit box with the new-found money. They will get this amount back, in any event, the mom is told.

The jolly threesome go to a bank, where both con women withdraw $1,000 apiece. They then proceed to the mom's bank, where they watch to make sure that the mom withdraws her money. Con woman A places this in an envelope with her funds and puts it all into her purse "for safekeeping."

From the bank, they may go to the lawyer's office, where they will hand over their money to the lawyer, who is in actuality a con man in league with the con women. He will set up a time for the mom to collect her share. By the date of her appointment, he will be long gone. Or the two con women may use any one of a number of dodges to ditch the mom. Con woman A may decide to go to the ladies' room and never return; she might ask the mom to please go and buy her a box of tampons, as if embarrassed, to which the mom will gladly assent; or she may say that she has to make a telephone call to her husband to see if her kids are all right. The mom, remembering the photographs and the story about the little boy who is sick, will probably not suspect anything until it's too late. Con woman B then goes off in search of con woman A, and the mom is left alone. By the time her nervousness gives way to the dreadful realization that she has been duped, the two women are far away, divvying up their loot.

Bank Examiner Swindle

In this con, usually perpetrated on older women, especially widows, the assumption is that widowed middle-class women generally have the proceeds from their husbands' life insurance policies deposited in the bank. The object of the bank swindle, of course, is to separate the old lady from this money.

This con requires research. One way of obtaining information is to stand in line at the teller's window at a bank, studying customers as they come and go, and noting account numbers and amounts of withdrawals and deposits. After selecting a victim, the con man calls her from a phone booth, explaining that he is a federal bank examiner who has been appointed to investigate possible teller dishonesty at her bank. Will she help the authorities apprehend the embezzler? All she need do is withdraw a specified amount of money from her account (sometimes the con man will advise her to wear gloves when she handles the money), place it in an envelope, and allow a bank officer to inspect the bills for fingerprints and serial numbers. She is told that the money will be immediately reimbursed to her account, and often a reward is offered.

If the woman agrees, the con may send a taxi to pick her up, or he and a confederate may chauffeur her in an expensive car. In another variation, the con men dress as police officers and drive a police car. Sometimes they will pretend to be undercover cops and flash appropriate IDs. In any case, the con men take off with the victim's money, which is, of course, never put back into her account, nor is the promised reward forthcoming.

Strange as it may seem, this con has worked extremely well on both the East and West Coasts for many years. Those taken in by the hoax simply do not suspect the fraudulent bank examiner until it is too late. Some, when questioned over the phone, actually get their bank books and obligingly read off their records to the caller. In Denver, where this scam recurs in cycles, a bunco squad officer remarked that the victims are motivated by greed. Perhaps. But it seems more likely that the mark's exaggerated and unrealistic respect for authority leads him or her to put faith in anyone who can play the part of "an important official."

Jamaican Handkerchief or Envelope Switch

This switch has countless variations, all of which feature the con man putting his money into some sort of covering or container with the mark's money, and then unobtrusively trading this parcel for another of similar appearance, usually bulked out with worthless paper. Any number of pretexts have been used for clubbing the two stashes. Traditionally, two con men, ostensibly strangers to one another, play this con against a mark.

In the Jamaican switch, the two cons are a *marblecake team:* One is black (originally impersonating a Jamaican, fresh off the boat) and the other white. This combination works to their advantage, allowing them to play both blacks and whites as opportunity allows. The "Jamaican" may alternatively pose as a sailor or other foreigner looking to have a good time in the city.

Con man A approaches his prospective mark and shows him an address printed on a piece of paper. He asks whether the man can tell him how to get to this place, and offers him fifty dollars for his help. Around this time, con man B happens along, and con man A asks him for directions, too. Con man B tells him not to show his money around, and pretends to give him advice about where to go for a good time.

"But it's not safe to go in there with all that money," he warns. "Better let me hold on to it for you."

Con man A refuses, saying that he trusts the other man— the mark—and wants him to hold on to his money for him. He pulls out a big wad of bills and wraps them in a white handkerchief. He then seems to doubt his action.

"I trust you, but I'm afraid you won't take care of this money like it was your own. Put your money in here, too, and then I know you'll protect it."

The mark does so and prepares to put the handkerchief into his pocket.

"No, no," one or both con men protest, "not like that! You have to carry it next to your heart." One of them demonstrates how the money should be carried and then hands back the handkerchief. The mark puts it inside his shirt as directed. Later he opens the handkerchief and discovers it is stuffed with pieces of newspaper.

Sometimes the con men persuade the mark to go to the bank and withdraw a sum of money equal to that which con man A has in his handkerchief to show "good faith" or ensure that he will guard the money as if all of it were his own. It should go without saying that any time a stranger asks you to withdraw funds from your account, for any reason, you should immediately begin to smell a rat!

Obituary Hustle

This particularly nasty type of confidence game owes its high success rate to the manipulation of a bereaved person's or family's grief. The con man or woman reads the obituary column in the newspaper where all the information pertinent to this scam is revealed: the names of the deceased and his survivors, their addresses, and sometimes other facts the con can use. There are many variations, but a common ploy is to impersonate a delivery person collecting for "this material that Mr. Appleton ordered." Usually the wife, husband, or family member will sign and pay for the package, no questions asked. The con may imply that the package, not yet paid for, contains a gift, back-ordered long ago, for the widow, and she will in most cases thankfully pay a high price to receive it. If it is jewelry, she may never know that it is inexpensive, because she won't have it appraised, and may never realize that she has been the victim of a hoax. There have been cases in which pornographic or other objectionable materials have been delivered under the same pretext.

Three-Card Monte

One of the oldest games around, three-card monte still works. An old man and one or two shills set up in a public park, and proceed to bet on a card-guessing game. The old man shuffles and deals the cards. He seemingly can't understand why one of the young men is always able to pick the red card, Queen of Spades, or whatever, out of the three cards he lays down. The old fellow loses money every time. A casual onlooker notices that one corner of the card so consistently identified by the young man has been bent. The shill winks at him, implicating him in the hoax, which the onlooker believes to be on the old man. The onlooker is encouraged to try his hand at three-card monte. Thinking he can't loose, he chooses the bent card, only to discover that it is a substitute for the original, and that he has lost his bet.

Poker Bunco

A well-known ploy also used in dice, pool, and other games, poker bunco continues to work despite its widespread notoriety.

Let's say that two men are playing a friendly game of poker. Unbeknownst to the man who is winning, his opponent is a cardsharp out to set him up. The con man congratulates the winner—we'll call him Paul—and tells him some stories about a wealthy, respectable citizen he knows who can't play cards worth a damn but who loves to gamble. Eventually, con man A arranges a game in a hotel room.

Sometimes the mark is put on the send for more money while he is still enjoying his winning streak to show he'd be good for the money if he started to lose. The blow-off is often an argument in which con man A accuses con man B of cheating, triggering the visit of the hotel keeper (an accomplice of the two con men) who orders them all out of the building with threats that he will call the police.

Missing-Heir Scheme

Have you ever wished that some long-lost relative would leave you his estate, complete with family jewels and polo ponies? Have you ever suspected that despite your prosaic family history, the blue blood of a dashing aristocratic ancestor pulses through your veins? If so, you are not alone. Inheriting wealth and prestige from an uncommon forebear is a common American dream, and one from which countless scammers have profited.

A mild form of this scheme is perpetrated by fly-by-night "geneologists," enterprising souls aided by word processors. Using the phone book, they send out thousands of letters offering to sell the recipient a book about his glorious roots. The price of this book is between twenty-five and fifty dollars, and those contacted are led to believe that it is all about their own family tree. In reality, the material is a conglomeration of useless information about many different family names, and much of the information is made up for the occasion.

One woman we know received such a letter. *Dear Mrs. OREEN,* it ran, *Send now for this high-quality volume wherein you will read of your ancestors, the fine old OREEN family* ... Mrs. Oreen promptly consigned the letter to the wastebasket, knowing that there never had been any such thing as a fine old Oreen family. Her husband's father, upon arriving in the United States from the old country, was given his surname by customs officials who found his true monicker too big a mouthful. "Oreen" was the closest they bothered to come to his fine old family name. Along the same lines, many people have been sold renderings of their so-called authentic family crests, only to discover later that their family never had a heraldic crest, shield, or coat of arms.

These computerized form letters advertising geneological

memorabilia are a spin-off of the venerable missing heir scheme, which is still going strong today. The modern version of this scam runs loosely as follows.

The victim receives either an official-looking letter or a phone call, informing him that he is the sole heir of a wealthy gentleman of the same surname. Let us say that the con man perpetrating the hoax in this case is wary of postal fraud charges and so chooses to locate his mark by phone.

"Mr. Bumpf," he states solemnly, "I am sorry to inform you that your relation, the late Mr. Horace X. Bumpf, has died intestate."

"Oh," replies the puzzled mark, "that's too bad."

"As you are of course aware," continues the con man, *"intestate* means that he had no will."

"Of course."

"I, as probate investigator, have learned that you stand to inherit Mr. Horace X. Bumpf's estate."

At this point the mark begins to say that he has never heard of anyone in his family named Horace, but decides against it. "Oh yeah?" he says.

"It is virtually indisputable. I think it is only fair to warn you that the inheritance tax will consume a large portion of the estate . . ."

The mark, who has never before given a thought to the inheritance tax, nor, for that matter, to Mr. Horace X. Bumpf, now curses this unjust encroachment of the IRS on his life.

". . . leaving you only approximately $2 million."

"Two million *dollars?"*

"Yes, that is correct. Approximately. Of course, in order to investigate further and to assure the protection of your rights under law, I will have to charge a fee of $50. This should be sent immediately . . ."

The mark sends his fee, buys a case of champagne, and then waits around to hear from the probate investigator. But he never does hear another word about his relation, the worthy Mr. Horace X. Bumpf, or his estate.

While the missing-heir scheme continues to be viable, no one has ever milked it as thoroughly as did Oscar Hartzell. Operating in the great American Heartland where he grew up, Hartzell and his confederates reaped more than $2 million between the years 1924 and 1932 with false promises of proceeds from the mythical Drake Estate.

Hartzell first learned about the Drake con the hard way. Two sharpers, a man and a woman, both with English accents, told his mother that she was one of the American heirs to a fabulous fortune left by the illegitimate son of Sir Francis Drake and Queen Elizabeth. The royal family, in an attempt to keep the lady monarch's indiscretion a secret, had been holding this fortune since the sixteenth century. If the American Drake descendants would donate what they could, the cons would continue their efforts to bring the skeleton out of the closet and distribute the inheritance which was so long overdue. Oscar was a boy at the time, but he realized intuitively that the Drake inheritance was a ruse. His mother saw it differently and sold her Madison County, Iowa, farm in order to help fund the two charlatans.

Another son might have devoted his life to protecting widows who had been tricked as his mother had been or to tracking down the con team to avenge her honor. Oscar did, in fact, track down the Drake heir duo, but for another reason. He wanted to get in on the action. First he collaborated with them, then cut them out by anonymously reporting them to Scotland Yard when he accompanied them to England. He was now the primary perpetrator of the Drake inheritance scam, and perpetrate he did.

Hartzell went from farm to farm, charming the people with his friendly, easygoing manner and the promise that he would increase any donations he received from Drake descendants one hundred to one. The fact that he, too, was a Midwestern farm boy gave him the in he needed, and he quickly gained the trust and support of a wide following. It was not difficult for Hartzell to convince the Anglo-Saxon population that so many of them were related to the offspring of the commander who defeated the Spanish Armada and the daughter of King Henry VIII of England. True, he admitted, this Drake was a bastard. Why else would the English Royal Family work so hard to keep him a secret all these years? And distribution of the fortune—roughly twenty-two billion dollars, including interest, according to Hartzell's calculations—would naturally throw the whole British economy out of kilter. No wonder the "interests" in England wanted to sit on Drake's rightful estate.

Eventually Hartzell became so successful that he had to hire salesmen. Trips to England, ostensibly to attack the "interests" and work for the farmers' legal rights to the Drake estate, were frequent. Thousands of devotees kept him amply supplied with funds, even after the authorities began to take note of him and to warn that contributors to the Drake cause would get nothing in return for their money. Hartzell had become a cult figure, and his fans were loyal. Just in case, however, Hartzell told them that any complaints to the authorities would exclude them from collecting on the Drake estate, once the British resistance had been overcome.

Hartzell was finally convicted of mail fraud and sent to Leavenworth, but most of his followers never did lose faith in him. They believed till the end that the people who put him in prison were responsible for bilking them out of their rightful inheritance.

Gold-Mine Swindle

Gold has always had an inducement for otherwise sensible people to go hog wild. The gold-mine swindle, a basically simple scam, was no doubt used by Spanish and English buccaneers and adventurers to the Americas long ago, and is still in evidence today. It is especially prevalent in the western United States when gold is selling high.

The con man lets it be known that he owns the rights to a discontinued gold mine capable of producing a wealth of ore. He requires a certain amount of money in order to work it and will sell shares to interested parties in order to do so. Sometimes he establishes himself in the church community, snares a well-respected clergyman in his web, and then allows him to lead the flock to the moose pasture. *(Moose pasture* is a term for worthless land or mineral rights or defunct mines.) Sometimes the shares are sold by boiler-room operations over the telephone.

While the gold-mine swindle can be worked as a short con, it is also frequently what is sometimes called a *long con,* a scam that can go on for years and years before the investors get wise to the swindler.

Spanish Prisoner Game

This con has been traced back as far as 1588 to the days when Philip II of Spain launched his Invincible Armada against England. Modern practitioners may claim to be prisoners in Central America, Mexico, or Vietnam, but the game is the same.

The victim is usually contacted by letter, although the con may present the letter in person. The message is purportedly from a fellow countryman held prisoner in a foreign land. He requires money in order to bribe his captors or pay a ransom. A treasure map or other supposedly valuable papers are often included as collateral, along with a picture of the prisoner's beautiful, languishing daughter. It is implied that she will be part of the contributor's reward for helping to free the captive. Other benefits include money and property, for the prisoner is always portrayed as an extremely wealthy man, capable of renumerating his savior once he is back on home soil. Businessmen are most frequently the victims of this hoax.

Murphy Game

The gist of this old, simple swindle is that a mark is conned into paying for basic services which he never receives. The Murphy game, also known as Miss Murphy, paddy hustle, or carpet game, allows a con man the monetary advantages of pimping while saving himself the aggravation of actually having to deal with employees.

The Murphy game is played in the parts of town where prostitution is practiced. The mark is told that he can have a girl for a certain number of hours for a certain fee. It is always a good deal, and the mark is generally given his choice of any race, age, or sexual specialty. Why not? The con man is in a position to be generous. He accepts the mark's money, tells the mark which door to go in and what to say and do, and he then disappears with the cash. By the time the mark realizes that there are no girls there, it is too late to get his money back.

There are many possible variations on this game. The con man may simply take the mark's money and tell him to "go on in there and say Charlie sent you" before he makes tracks. He may explain that the girls are all very clean and that customers must have a routine VD checkup by a nurse before being allowed into the rooms. The mark hands over his money and goes into a restroom to await the nurse while the con man catches a cab for the other side of town. Another alternative is for the con man to ask to see the money to make sure that the mark has enough and then feign concern that someone might steal him blind. The con man reminds the mark that he is in a bad neighborhood, and the mark, already keenly aware of this fact and somewhat nervous about it, is willing to take suggestions.

"Tell you what you do," the con man says, pulling an envelope from his own pocket. "You put all your money in here and then hand it to the desk clerk at the hotel. He'll take out what you owe and hold the rest till you come out so that nobody steals it from you."

The mark does as directed. The con man then reaches into his pocket for a pen and puts the amount the mark owes on the outside of the envelope. He also writes down the amount the desk clerk will give him back.

When the mark asks the desk clerk about the girls, he is told that there are no prostitutes on the premises. The mark looks inside the envelope and finds only strips of newspaper; the con man has pulled a switch.

The Murphy game is played on servicemen, young men and boys out looking for a good time, conventioneers, and other likely candidates.

Badger Game

The badger game, or refined Miss Murphy, is worked on the same likely candidates as in the previous scam with the exception that in some versions the mark must be in the area for more than one night.

The *badger* is a con woman or prostitute who is in on the scam. She plays the part of a married woman looking for some excitement but afraid that her husband will find out about her fling. She may allow the mark to come to her apartment the next morning after an evening of drinking at a bar, or she may string him along for several days before allowing him to go to bed with her. Once they are alone together, she asks her "date" to get undressed in the adjoining room and then come into the bedroom. She will be clever enough to find some pretext for disrobing in some other part of the house than that in which the final intimacies are to take place. While she and the mark are engaged in the bedroom, her coworker will be removing all the money, credit cards, and other valuables from his pockets.

Another variation of this game is for her partner, playing the part of a jealous husband, to break in on the lovebirds and threaten them with death, dismemberment, or a phone call to the mark's wife, should he happen to be married. In the ensuing confusion, the mark will often hand over any money he has brought with him and can then be blackmailed for the rest.

5.

In the Privacy of Your Own Home

Caveat Emptor. (Let the buyer beware.)
Roman proverb

If your home is your castle, why are you bothered by door-to-door salesmen pitching everything from blacktop to eternal salvation? Why does your mailbox overflow with amazing offers, which if accepted will only leave you deeper in debt? Why do strangers call you up conducting "surveys" and pitching swampland in Florida? Short of moving to the backwoods, we know of no foolproof way to avoid such intrusions. They are as much a part of our way of life as the common cold or gastrointestinal flu. But you can keep ahead of hucksters and scammers by becoming familiar with their methods.

DOOR-TO-DOOR CONS

You can throw junk mail in the trash and hang up on telephone solicitors, but the door-to-door salesman is more troublesome. If he gets you cornered in your yard or gets a foot in your door, he is difficult to discourage. In the old days, castle-dwellers used to hire people to pour boiling oil or molten lead on intruders, but presumably we live in more enlightened times. It just isn't that easy anymore; we are forced to rely on common sense. While common sense is less exciting than boiling lead, it is a great deal neater, and just as effective in most cases.

Home Repair

It was a beautiful day in early May. Frank Miller was out in his front yard with a wheelbarrow and shovel, spreading cow manure on his wife's garden. He and Sally had just bought their first home and had begun to realize that owning a house was going to be an expensive proposition. It was an old house in a quiet residential neighborhood. The Millers had been so glad to find a place they could afford—or almost afford—that they overlooked a few flaws when the realtor showed them around. Already Frank had paid for rewiring and plumbing repairs and had replaced the rotten porch rail by himself. When the spring thaw brought April showers, the Millers discovered to their dismay that the roof leaked, but they didn't have enough money to get it fixed. When a pleasant, freckle-faced kid came up and proposed a low-budget, roof-repair job, Frank thought it was his lucky day.

The kid explained that his dad, a building contractor, had been working on someone else's house in the neighborhood and just happened to have some materials left over.

"Would you be interested in having some repairs done for the cost of materials, sir?" he asked.

Frank looked over across the street, where a shiny, late-model Ford pickup truck sat idling at the curb. The driver, a clean-shaven, friendly looking sort, waved when he caught Frank's eye. Frank enthusiastically motioned for him to come over and talk.

Bill Williamson, the contractor, was a man who inspired confidence; at least, Frank trusted him right away. He was tall and carried himself with easy self-assurance. He was, as Frank later told police, someone who could look you in the eye.

Yes, Bill said, he and the boy here had been doing some weekend remodel work. The boy was just a chip off the old block. But now they had all these materials left over, and he was going to have to eat them, as he put it, unless he used them up. He was willing to work cheap.

"Well, this is certainly a coincidence," Sally said, trowel in hand. She was beaming at Bill's son—such a courteous, well-groomed child for his age! "Our roof has been leaking for weeks, but we haven't been able to afford to have it fixed."

"Oh, not such a coincidence," Bill told her pleasantly, idly batting at a spiraling bumblebee. "These older houses do that. This time of year, everybody all of a sudden wants a carpenter. We've been booked solid. Getting so it's pretty near impossible for a homeowner to get work done, at any price. But, as I say, we just happened to be in the neighborhood . . ."

The first price Bill bid was so low that Frank was embarrassed to have to turn it down. "We're just really strapped for money," he said. "I wouldn't ask you to take anything less, but—"

No, no, Bill reassured him, he could go a little lower. Otherwise, as he'd mentioned earlier, he'd just have to eat the cost of the materials. Furthermore, Williamson Construction absolutely guaranteed all work for one year after completion. "Company policy," Bill said.

As it later came to light, Frank wasn't the only one spreading manure around that day. After the roofing job was completed, it began to rain. And when Frank and Sally went inside, congratulating themselves for getting the repairs finished just, as they thought, in the nick of time, they found that the leaks had not been fixed at all. After the thunderstorm had passed, Frank got up on the roof and discovered that Bill had merely coated portions of it with crankcase oil.

Frank and Sally had been victims of the infamous Williamson gang. At least there was some comfort in numbers: All over town, gang members had been swarming around all day, making so-called repairs. At about four o'clock, as if by pre-arranged schedule, they had climbed into their trucks and disappeared like a plague of locusts. Law-enforcement officials had no way of knowing where they would show up next. Some people had agreed to have their driveways blacktopped, only to discover, with the downpour, that crankcase oil had been used. Others had been shown bits of termite-infested wood, purportedly taken from their own homes but actually smuggled in by the Williamsons. Some had paid for "state of the art" paint jobs; now their exterior walls, washed by rain, had regained their usual lackluster appearance, and the paint lay in puddles in their yards. Others had paid for tree-planting. They would not realize until a week or so later that sawn branches, not saplings, had been planted in their lawns. Like the fly-by-night Williamsons, these "trees" would never take root.

The Williamson gang is real. A family-based, organized criminal community, the gang supposedly numbers about 5,000 according to police estimates. While not all of the Williamson gang families are actually Williamsons, most are in fact interrelated by blood. Other common surnames are Stewart, McGavin, McDonald, McMillan, Boswell, Keith, Parks, Reid, and Johnson. Nomads, they stay in trailer parks, taking to the interstates in their well-kept vehicles to roam the nation in search of new victims. When one member of the gang is picked up by law-enforcement officials, the others all seem to know about it instantly and quickly disperse. Some say that it's their Celtic blood that enables them to communicate telepathically; others think they use wrist radios and CBs. Whatever their methods may be, they are clannish in the extreme, and usually manage to bail each other out of trouble.

While the Williamsons live like gypsies, they are not gypsies in the strict sense. The Williamsons are of British descent, and arrived in this country around the turn of the century. Their pattern was established and recognized soon after, when police began to notice that the name *Williamson* kept cropping up in cases involving fraud, deception, and confidence scams.

A recent Williamson con involves the sale of substandard trailers, glossed up and resold under deceptive pretenses as high-quality vehicles. Williamson salesmen are excellent ad-libbers. The usual line is that, while they hate to let the trailers go, a death in the family or other tragedy is forcing them to sell at a loss. Beware the man selling travel trailers with the brand names Buccaneer, Hornet, Impala, Lamath, Lariat, La Salle, Majestic, Monte Carlo, Rogue, Sunbeam, Tropicana, Shenandoah, or Spartan. Chances are good you're up against a Williamson. He is likely to tell you that the vehicles are under full warranty which will be honored by any recreational vehicle dealer, but such is not the case. Many dealers will not work on a trailer that has substandard insulation, plumbing, or wiring, or which does not meet state standards.

Law authorities in California have established a physical description of Williamson gang members. While this description is, of course, very general, it gives an overall picture of what to expect. All gang members are white and of British descent. Men are usually tall, from five feet ten inches to six feet five inches in height, and muscular. They are clean-shaven or mustached. Women are usually slender, tall, and well-dressed. Children are often neater, cleaner, and more outwardly respectful of adults than the norm. They are family-oriented, and travel in well-cared-for, late-model vehicles, especially pickup trucks.

When engaged in the home-repair racket, the Williamsons' M.O. is to hit on retired or elderly homeowners, especially widows, with sufficient funds to pay for improvements. They are, however, willing to rip off anyone outside of their own group, regardless of age, sex, or employment status, if they think there's good money to be made.

The Williamsons are not the only perpetrators of home-repair fraud. There are plenty of other scammers out there who pose as honest carpenters, odd-jobbers, electricians, and furnace repairmen in order to scam homeowners. The story of Rosabel Penny and Ron Lee Jones, taken from Denver police records, illustrates how the old furnace-repair con operates.

Our story begins with police officer Joe R. Rousseau, as he pulls over a speeder and asks him for his license. The license, in the name of Charles A. Bryan, was forthcoming, but Rousseau quickly recognized it as a fake. When the self-styled Mr. Bryan was confronted with the dubious authenticity of this document, he readily handed over another, in the name of Ron Lee Jones. "But," wrote Rousseau in his log, "I have determined this ID also to be phony."

The motorist, whom we'll call Ron Lee for lack of exact data, was taken to the station. Rousseau connected him with a bad check written out to Ron Lee Jones by an elderly lady named Rosabel Penny. Miss Penny had made out the amount for $200; Jones had "improved" it to read $900. Not much was found out about Jones' background or true identity, and he was not particularly generous with information that might produce any clues as to his real identity. "Doesn't know where he comes from," state the police records. The suspect did admit to having a wife and eight children "whereabouts unknown." Even for a con man it must be hard to lose a wife and eight children. But, to get back to the story: Why did Rosabel Penny write him that check?

Apparently Ron Lee Jones had been running a furnace-repair scam, a type of swindle frequently perpetrated in established middle-class neighborhoods where most residents are homeowners. The presumption made by the con man is that a longtime resident of such a neighborhood will own an old furnace, which he or she can be convinced to replace. The con artist, posing as a health inspector, utility company employee, or other trustworthy type, perhaps wearing a snappy uniform for the sake of credibility, knocks at the door and asks to be allowed in to perform a safety check on the furnace. He will act businesslike and sincerely concerned about the welfare of the homeowner. Of course, there will be no charge for this service.

Once inside, the con artist pretends to inspect the furnace. After some fooling around, scowling, and head shaking, he announces that the old junker is on its last legs. It's just a matter of time before it goes off like a bomb, blowing the house sky-high. Or maybe it is the insidious kind, slowly filling the house with deadly vapors.

"To be perfectly honest, ma'am, I'm surprised it's lasted this long. Far as I can tell, you're just living on borrowed time with this model. When did you say you bought it? Yep, that's what I thought. I hate to tell you this, but this old baby's gonna blow. Might be ten months from now, might be ten minutes."

Fortunately for the homeowner, he says, he just happens to have access to an excellent model that he can sell at cost. If the homeowner is not sufficiently terrified to agree immediately, he uses one of several tricks to show that the casing is cracked, parts are rusted, or whatever. Because very few people are up on the price of new furnaces, he is often able to charge a monstrously inflated amount without arousing suspicion. He collects his money for the new model, which he may or may not deliver. If he does deliver it, it will be a cheap one, probably inferior to the furnace it replaces.

So that is the con the alleged Ron Lee allegedly pulled on Rosabel Penny. He got caught when her personal check was questioned at the bank, and Miss Penny, unlike many a confidence victim, decided to press charges. At this writing, Ron

Lee's case has not yet come to trial. Assuming that he is still in the vicinity when his case comes up, will he be enough of a con artist to persuade the jury to let him off? His skill will have to be considerable to tip the scales against a plaintiff like Rosabel Penny.

If you own your house, you should be careful of home-repair swindlers. Be suspicious when:

- a construction crew arrives with "leftover materials" and offers to give you a good deal.
- you are approached after fire, high winds, or water has damaged your home by someone who quotes you a price for repairs.
- any representative of a home-improvement outfit solicits you, either over the phone or door-to-door. Some legitimate businesses operate this way, especially if they are just getting established and need to hustle for business, but most rely on word of mouth and their reputation to generate customers.
- a construction company offers you a bargain on aluminum siding, painting, or other "improvements" in order to use your house as a showplace for their work. This is an old con, but it's still effective.
- a so-called public service employee, or anyone else, offers a free furnace, chimney, vermin, or wiring inspection. If they tell you that they represent a company you know and trust, call that company and get the facts; also check any references you are given. And ask the operator for the number or look it up yourself in the phone book. In all too many instances, an individual will be careful enough to call, but will accept the phone number supplied by the con man. This is, of course, the number of a pay phone or public place where an accomplice is waiting to pick up the phone.
- you are offered any deal that sounds too good to be true.

Could I Have Just a Moment of Your Time?

Dagwood Bumstead's method of dealing with door-to-door hucksters has always been to send them flying off his front stoop with a well-placed kick in the pants. While this is undoubtedly the most emotionally gratifying way to dispose of a persistent salesman, it tends to encourage him to file charges of assault and battery, and is therefore not advisable. It is preferable to say "no" immediately, cutting him off in midspiel, and to close the door quickly before he can wedge a foot in.

Magazine, encyclopedia, vacuum cleaner, and other door-to-door sales are often out-and-out frauds. Even when you do receive the product you have been promised, it is almost certain to be overpriced. The beauty of the door-to-door sales method for the con man is that it allows him to use his most devastating weapon, his gift of persuasion, collect money, and disappear before the mark gets wise. There is a fine line between legitimate high-pressure sales techniques and fraud. Aside from a few reputable companies like Fuller Brush, Avon, and the Girl Scouts, most businesses that pitch their wares door-to-door are not to be trusted. If you are in the market for a product, rather than buying from a door-to-door salesman, you will do better to seek out reputable businesses that deal in the line in which you are interested.

In one documented case, an attorney general's investigator asked a homeowner's cooperation in nailing a company suspected of fraudulent dealings. The homeowner was told about the misrepresentations and outright lies allegedly used to solicit sales. He was asked to invite a salesman from the suspect company to his home and then to record the ensuing conversation on a hidden tape recorder. After the pitch had been delivered, the homeowner was told to decline the offer. The investigator was amazed to find that, despite his briefing, the homeowner had signed the contract as directed by the salesman. When the investigator asked him why he had signed even when he knew he was being conned, the embarrassed homeowner mumbled that he had been unable to resist "such a good deal." This is a typical case of the amateur consumer up against the professional salesman. (You'll save yourself a lot of trouble if you refuse to put yourself in the position to be ripped off.)

Be on your guard when you encounter any of the following warning signs—you may be dealing with a con man or con woman.

- A delivery person asks you to pay a C.O.D. charge on a package you are not expecting, and you don't recognize the return address on the package. You may be asked to pay for a package for a family member or neighbor when he is not at home. This is a frequently used con. When the box is opened it is discovered that it contains a brick or other worthless material.

- Goods are delivered that were supposedly ordered by a recently deceased family member. "Obit cons" are practiced by ghouls who read the obituary columns every day and then perpetrate cons on the survivors. Carefully check out any such "debts" before paying.

- You are asked, either over the phone or at your door, to contribute to a charity of which you have no knowledge. Many times the name of a bogus charity is deliberately designed to resemble that of a bona fide one. Have the representative send you information through the mail; if the cause appeals to you, check out the organization before contributing. One common example of the charity bunco is the company, or companies, that imitate a respectable charity that sells light bulbs in order to help the blind. There are countless other operations, both small and large, that thrive by preying on the public's charitable instincts—or, in some cases, on the public's desire for a tax deduction.

- A salesperson requests your "help" to take a trip or win a scholarship. This is a fraudulent sales technique commonly used in door-to-door sales of national magazines. Usually such salespersons are the young, underpaid hirelings of a fat-cat con man. Their pitch is carefully rehearsed, but has little or no factual information. Prices are inflated, and your chances of ever receiving the subscriptions you pay for are slim to none. Because the distributor is out of state and the salesperson is difficult to locate, those who pay up front and receive no magazines are unlikely to get their money back.
- You are offered a promotional free prize. There are always strings attached. The prize is bait intended to pull you into a scam or sales scheme, and is not actually free; at least, not if the prize-issuer can help it.
- Be wary any time you are offered any kind of deal on encyclopedias by a door-to-door salesperson. The pitch is engineered to make you feel that you are getting a real bargain; the salesperson will play on your emotions. Your insecurities about your own education or concern for your children can be manipulated. By the time you sign the contract, the "bargain" has become a long-term obligation. Those who really want an encyclopedia will save hundreds of dollars by ordering an up-to-date set directly from the publisher. Remember: Door-to-door encyclopedia sales is a scammy business.
- You are asked to write a check with the promise that you can call the next day and get your money back if you change your mind. Any money you put into a con-artist's hand is long-gone.

If you have allowed a door-to-door salesperson into your home, be suspicious (or even belligerent) when:
- a salesperson attempts to manipulate you emotionally, through your own sympathy, insecurity, prejudice, or

greed. This is the oldest trick in the book—and a highly effective one—for putting the mark off balance and, consequently, easier to fleece.

- you are hurried into signing a contract with an "act now or miss this sterling opportunity" pitch. Always take time to know exactly what you are doing. The con artist wants you to act on impulse, while you're still under his guidance. If the deal is legitimate, the salesperson won't push you to sign before you've had time to consult friends, the Better Business Bureau, a lawyer, your husband or wife, or whoever.

- a salesperson seemingly does not want you to carefully read and understand the contract in its entirety—especially the fine print. He may ask you to sign what he calls an authorization or a statement, which confirms that he has talked with you, so that he "won't get in trouble with the boss." Many people are surprised to find, weeks later, that they have signed a contract which obliges them to pay large sums of money due to fraudulent misrepresentation on the part of sales people. They may have no recourse, however, because such swindlers will sell the contracts they obtain by dishonest means to finance companies at a discount. The finance company will try its damnedest to squeeze the payments out of you after the slick operator is long gone.

- a salesperson in your home does not inform you of your legal three-day right to cancel any contract you sign on your premises. This law was enacted to protect the public against swindlers, frauds, con artists, and their brethren, but is not commonly known. It is the salesperson's responsibility to inform you of it.

If you have been conned, or if you suspect that someone has attempted to swindle you, contact your Better Business Bureau, police department, and attorney general's office. Or, if you feel you must and he hasn't already slithered away, boot the creep off your front stoop.

TELEPHONE SCAMS: BOILER-ROOM FRAUD IN THE EIGHTIES

Spawned during the 1920s as a way to sell worthless stock, the boiler-room—a telephone sales office from which the con man works—has come of age. Luxurious and well appointed, most boiler-room offices are merely hole-in-the-wall operations—low-rent offices equipped with lots of telephones and staffed with aggressive sales personnel.

The perfect medium for the well-spoken con artist, the telephone allows him to save the time and energy it would take to canvas neighborhoods for investors. Even more important, the telephone connects him with an unlimited number of prospective marks across the nation.

Another plus for the con artist is the mobility afforded by the boiler room. Operators need not keep up appearances by maintaining an impressive office or sporting fashionable clothes; their customers never see them or their work space. Thus operators remain anonymous, and a bare-bones approach to office furnishings can be taken. The result is that when law-enforcement officials get wise to the fraudulent nature of an enterprise, operators can quickly pack and set up shop somewhere else under a different name. The business address is generally not made public, so it takes the law a while to sniff out the new location. The operators thus gain themselves some time for escape-and-evasion purposes, while keeping their identity secret.

Taking advantage of these factors, unscrupulous operators have in recent years used the boiler room as a headquarters for the dissemination of various cons, notably oil-lease, gold, and office supply swindles.

Most boiler-room operations are located in the Sun Belt.

The con artist depends on the elderly the way an animal predator depends on field mice: They are his primary means of sustenance, even though he will occasionally go after more challenging game. Large populations of retired people congregating in Florida, Arizona, and California make these states prime hunting grounds. When authorities concentrate law-enforcement efforts on busting mom-and-pop con artists, many such con men turn to *telemarketing*, a fancy name for reaching out and putting the touch on someone.

Of all the boiler-room operation centers, Florida ranks number one. Besides a large cadre of con men as described above, the Sunshine State boasts a highly mobile army of sales personnel trained in the fine old tradition of land-sale fraud. Sales techniques developed during the Fifties and Sixties for the purpose of encouraging would-be homeowners from out of state to purchase swampland readily lend themselves to all kinds of boiler-room scams. With its big, savvy labor pool and its tradition of skullduggery, Florida is a natural operational base for dishonest telemarketers.

The vital drug-smuggling business along Florida's coast and its high homicide and robbery rates divert police attention from white-collar crime. Under the circumstances, there is neither time nor money to adequately cope with nonviolent rip-offs. Furthermore, the Cayman Islands, only an hour away by air, provide a sort of tropical Switzerland for those who desire confidentiality in their financial affairs. Cayman banks will not release information on private accounts to authorities and are thus excellent hiding places for ill-gotten funds. When the going gets tough in Florida, the tough get going to the Cayman banks to stash their profits. The swindler can then close down shop and declare bankruptcy, thereby avoiding paying both the IRS and any investors.

Goat Pasture Scam

Picture this: You've just had a hard day at work. You go

into the kitchen to get a beer. The phone is ringing off the hook, and you decide to answer it. The caller immediately begins a prepared speech, difficult to interrupt. His voice is suave and businesslike. You could just hang up, but instead you listen awhile. His spiel goes as follows:

Hello! This is Ned, calling from the Famous Geological Oil & Gas Service. I'd like to give you some inside information on the latest developments in our oil and gas lease program. Have you heard of us?

Well, don't feel too bad. Most people don't even know there is such a service. In a nutshell, the U.S. Bureau of Land Management (BLM) sponsors a lottery for mineral rights—and that includes oil and natural gas—on federal land. In each drawing there are approximately 1,200 parcels, so each time 1,200 people just like you are winners.

Our geological advisory service is considered the Rolls Royce of our industry. The federal government hires us to remove the risk of the lottery for private customers like you. So we arrange a program of thirty recommended parcels in thirty drawings over the course of a year. All have been carefully researched and evaluated by our qualified geologists so that when you do win a lease, you will sell it right away to one of the big companies for megabucks! Let me say this: You will get a lease. What if, by some fluke, you can't sell the lease? Famous will buy it from you. We guarantee that absolutely.

Drilling will start almost immediately, and then you will receive a percentage of the income in royalty payments of many thousands of dollars. The minimum investment is $9,000, and that is 100 percent tax deductible—so, in essence, you are earning income with your tax dollars that would normally go into Uncle Sam's pocket. . . .

As you listen to the well-modulated voice, which rises and falls in volume with the professional precision of a radio announcer's, you imagine what the guy at the other end of the line looks like. You're tired, you've been knocking back that brew pretty fast, and you've got a good imagination. Even at that, you probably won't come close; in this case, truth is stranger than fiction. Let's adjourn for a moment to the boiler room and see for ourselves.

As Ned gives you his oil-lease pitch, he paces back and forth, phone receiver clamped to his bare shoulder, hands jammed under his armpits, and waves his elbows up and down in a sort of frantic chicken imitation. This is called *flapping* in boiler-room lingo. Because phone solicitors, or *yacks*, are thought to be most effective when they are both tired and excited, they frequently indulge in this exercise to get their blood pressure up. Coffee and cigarettes are popular among yacks because caffeine and nicotine enhance the hectic pace of the boiler-room environment. Although Ned sounds as if he should be wearing a suit and tie, he is casually attired in cut-off jeans and shower thongs. All around him other yacks, both men and women, are engaged in phone conversations similar to the one you are hearing.

Suddenly a man in full gorilla costume bounds into the room, shrieking and beating his chest. He performs a few antics, then bounds out again, slamming the door behind him. This was the manager. The week before, he circled the room on a souped-up Harley Davidson. The manager works hard at thinking of new ways to increase productivity by getting the yacks all hyped up. Every so often a bell rings, signaling that another sale has been made. Several happy yacks who have just earned themselves commissions go out into the hall for their cocaine break. They discuss the *mooches* (suckers) and *laydowns* (mooches who bit right away) to whom they have just sold some *goat pasture* (land with worthless mineral rights). Working a six-hour day, yacks average $30,000 in annual commissions.

These guys have learned a lot from their sales training sessions, specifically designed to assist yacks in boiler-room sales. They have learned even more from experience. They know, for instance, that most objections raised by mooches are not unanswerable, and can in fact even be anticipated. They have lists of commonly asked questions with appropriate replies, which are rattled off at a moment's notice. They also know that the best customers are those who have recently invested, and will contact them again and again until the mooches have been milked dry. Sucker lists are also exchanged among boiler-room companies in order to systematically work the repeaters.

Meanwhile, Ned is still yacking, and the noise in the office has grown even louder. The manager is announcing over the intercom that he will give twenty dollars to the person who makes the next sale. A few coked-up yacks, now reentering the room, howl in reply. You don't hear any of this background noise, though, because the phones are equipped with *confidencers,* devices that eliminate all of the sounds in the boiler room except for the salesman's voice.

Maybe you don't suspect that any of this insanity is taking place at the other end of the line, but you're not so bleary from a day's work and one beer that you will fall for a sales pitch like this one.

"If I could make you rich within four to six weeks for the price of your tax payment to the IRS, would you be interested?"

"Sounds too good to be true," you say.

"Sir, it is good, and it is true."

"Thanks anyway." You hang up.

Thousands, unfortunately, do not hang up—not before they have squandered their savings on a scam without checking the facts. Like any con artist worth his salt, the yack mixes as much truth as possible with his lies and misrepresentations. That way the mooch is more likely to believe everything he says. The U.S. Bureau of Land Management does in fact hold an oil-lease lottery on parcels of government land, and there are legitimate advisory services that will give an individual the benefit of their expertise for a fee.

How the Oil-Lease Lottery Works—Legitimately

> *It doesn't matter how well educated a person is, or how carefully you explain the risks involved in the lottery. He thinks he's automatically going to get rich. He just can't get past his big, bullshit dream.*
>   Industrial oil-and-gas lease consultant
>   Name withheld by request

You can enter the Bureau of Land Management oil-and-gas-lease lottery as an individual if you choose to do so. The entry fee is $75 for each parcel on which you bid. If you enter through a middleman company, you will sometimes pay up to $400 a parcel merely to enter. Acreage varies between parcels, but the entry fee is the same regardless of size. You must also pay a *delay rental fee* when you bid on a parcel. This fee equals the cost of one year's lease on the mineral rights of the property ($1 per acre). For example, if you bid on an eighty-acre parcel, your delay rental fee is $80.

If you don't win, your delay rental fee is returned, but your entry fee is forfeited. *If you do win*, though, you have contracted to lease the mineral rights on a specific piece of property for ten years at $1 per acre per year. The oil reserves under this land may be capable of supporting a productive oil well, and they may not. Geologists and others with expertise in the oil business can make educated guesses, but there is really no way to know for sure how much oil you're sitting on before drilling takes place. You will want to sell your lease to a large company, or you will otherwise be left holding the bag, paying $1 an acre every year for the next ten years on your goat pasture.

If a large company does buy your parcel, you will make a profit right away. Having paid $1 per acre on your lease, you might later sell the lease for $100 per acre, plus royalties of between 4 and 6 percent. You will be paid these royalties for as long as the site is in production, even if that period of time exceeds ten years. If the site proves to be a large oil reserve with productive wells, you'll be doing okay.

One way of choosing which parcel or parcels to bid on is to find out which are considered to have the greatest production potential. Land in an area known to be oil-rich is a good bet, although it is not certain even then that drilling will be profitable on your particular piece of property. There are going to be lots of bidders on parcels in highly productive areas, so your chances of winning such a drawing will be slight.

A parcel may be desired by a big company because it adjoins land owned by the company, land that is planned for, or currently under, development. Often government land will partially surround privately owned land on which drilling is taking place.

Like any other lottery, the oil-lease lottery is highly speculative. You could get rich. Some people do; entrepreneurs and little old ladies on Social Security alike have been known to make their fortunes through this lottery. Some people with expertise and experience in the oil business make their living by speculating in the lottery. Others lose their investments and never make a complete financial recovery.

The salesman from Famous Geological Oil & Gas Service, quoted above, was lying when he said that 1) his company was hired by the federal government to take the risk out of the program for individuals; 2) qualified geologists evaluated the Famous program; 3) you would definitely get a lease; and 4) your investment in the lottery would be tax deductible. If you do not win a lease, you can claim a capital loss. Your investment is actually tax deductible only if you own mineral rights, or if you have a working interest, like stock ownership, in a drilling site.

If you need professional advice when entering the U.S. Bureau of Land Management oil-lease lottery, seek out a reputable consultant. Don't contract with anyone who promises a no-risk investment, a surefire get-rich-quick scheme, or a tax deduction for your entry costs.

U.S. Oil and Gas

> These were crass people. They'd sell their own mother. And if their mother was already sold, they'd go out and buy another mother and sell her at a profit.
>
> James Bennett
> former U.S. Oil and Gas phone salesman
> From testimony before a federal grand jury.

Between September 1982 and June 1983, when law-enforcement officials stepped in, 66,000 eager mooches laid out approximately $8,784 apiece for the chance to win a $25,000 oil lease through U.S. Oil and Gas. Although boiler-room operators insisted that it was a sure thing, only sixty of the 66,000 won leases. Of the $8,784 entrance fee, $3,600 went to the U.S. Bureau of Land Management for filing fees, $1,600 went to the salesman's commission, and the balance, $3,584, went to U.S. Oil and Gas. Customers were told that they were bidding on forty-eight parcels, competing with about six to eight other potential buyers per parcel, but in fact one thousand or more people were in competition for each parcel.

Gurdon Wolfson, owner of U.S. Oil and Gas, was indicted

for fraud and conspiracy, and pleaded not guilty. During the 1960s, he had been an employee of Gulf American Properties, a company that was later censured by the Florida Land Sales Board for teaching salesmen to mislead investors. Telephone solicitors at U.S. Oil and Gas were apparently of the same school. Mark Douglas, a former U.S. Oil and Gas employee, testified that he made good money—about $500,000 a year by his own account—by using various imaginative sales pitches over the telephone. In his "Reagan pitch," he assured customers that they would win because the company had bribed the Reagan administration with $1 million in return for fixing 10 percent of its oil-lease lotteries.

Many people phoned by U.S. Oil and Gas solicitors contacted the Better Business Bureau. Some were surprised to hear that the company had a flawless record. As it happened, Henry Harris, president of the South Florida Better Business Bureau, a man who had often stated that he had no sympathy for people greedy enough to fall for boiler-room scams, was later indicted for accepting bribes from U.S. Oil and Gas to keep its file clean.

Westchase Oil-Lease Scam

While dozens of boiler-room operations used the government oil-lease lottery as a base for their schemes, Westchase did them all one better; it sold rights on land that the U.S. Bureau of Land Management did not consider worthy of placing in the lottery! Howard A. Malkin, Westchase president, allegedly purchased leases over the counter from the BLM. (Officials at the BLM state that it sells no leases for land thought to be near oil and gas reserves in this way.) In 1983 and 1984, oil and gas leases on forty-acre parcels of this land were sold to customers for $100 an acre, or twenty times what Westchase had paid for them. Telephone solicitors pitched the leases, stressing the supposed mineral wealth of the parcels, which were located in the Rocky Mountain Overthrust Belt Geologic area. One man was contacted by a saleswoman who said that she was calling from Denver. She asked him to wire Westchase $8,000 right away, promising him returns of $100,000 within forty days. He instead requested a brochure from the company, in which he read enough disclaimers to sour him on the deal. Others were told that they were winners of a federal oil-and-gas-lease lottery, giving them the opportunity to buy a guaranteed lease on land near wells pumping one thousand gallons a day. All they had to do was wire funds to Westchase for government closing costs.

Calling such statements "fraudulent misrepresentations," the FBI and cooperating law enforcement agencies seized over $184,000 from a Westchase bank account in Denver and closed the operation down. More Westchase funds were traced to a bank in Jacksonville, Florida.

Malkin was formerly the Florida agent for Trans-World Resources of Hollywood Corporation, a Florida-based oil-lease boiler-room operation. Trans-World was ordered to cease business in 1983 by Florida Comptroller Gerald A. Lewis, on the grounds that, with thirty other cited companies, it had defrauded thousands of investors across the country of millions of dollars.

Gold Scams

Gold has always been esteemed by cultures all over the world. Although its market price fluctuates, it is expected to hold its value, no matter what the dollar does, through troubled times, perhaps even nuclear holocaust. This quality, known as *liquidity*, makes gold very popular among investors. There are various ways to invest in gold, but buying the metal in the form of coins or bullion is considered safest, as the investor is buying a product of enduring value rather than speculating. It is important to get clear title to the gold right away.

In 1983, two precious metals firms collapsed, together leaving investors out $100 million. One of these firms, Bullion Reserve of North America, was based in Los Angeles, California; the other, International Gold Bullion Exchange (IGBE), operated out of Fort Lauderdale, Florida. Both had sold gold bullion by phone solicitation, television, and radio. The IGBE, the biggest gold and silver dealer in the United States, had sales of over $80 million in 1982.

Bullion Reserve was owned by Chairman Alan Saxon; IGBE by the Alderdice brothers, William and James. Following the collapse of the two companies, tragedy struck the owners. Alan Saxon killed himself the night before he was due to testify before a grand jury in New York. The story is that he left a suicide confession on his tape recorder, then ran a hose from his motorscooter exhaust pipe into the sauna, where he died of carbon monoxide poisoning. William Alderdice, the elder of the two brothers and president of IGBE, is also dead, murdered July 15, 1984, presumably in an argument over use of his car.

Bullion Reserve

Gold bullion may be the safest way to buy gold, but it is hardly the most convenient. It must be delivered by armored car, a costly kind of transportation, and it is difficult to store with any degree of security. One means of dealing with these difficulties is to pay a small fee to have your bullion warehoused. You never actually lay hands on the gold itself, but receive a negotiable warehouse receipt, which can be bought and sold. Such receipts are considered sounder currency than U.S. legal tender, as they are backed by gold. Alan Saxon took advantage of this practice by selling bullion, which he supposedly warehoused for investors in "nuclear-proof vaults in the Rocky Mountains." When the company failed, investigators discovered that of the $61 million which should have been in the vault, there was only $1 million in bullion. It is highly unlikely that the 30,000 customers bilked by Bullion Reserve will see their investments again.

International Gold Bullion Exchange

The IGBE salesmen were very, very nice over the phone. I said, "If anything's wrong with your company, please tell me." They said they certainly would.

Anonymous woman who invested with IGBE

The Alderdice brothers had tried many ways to make money before they hit on IGBE in 1979: everything from a wig salon to a penny arcade to a coin shop in a shopping mall. Gold bullion sales were an inspiration. With inflation increasing at a fantastic rate month by month, buying gold was considered a good way to protect one's money from losing its value. The Alderdices offered discounts on gold, with the stipulation that customers would wait from twelve to fifteen weeks for their bullion after payment. During this time, they would be paid 1.5 percent interest on their investment. (This system, known as *deferred delivery commodity option*, has been illegal since 1978, yet boiler-room operations continue to push the deferred delivery in many scams.) At first, there were actual gold bullion sales, but this was never the strong money-making angle of the company. After IGBE folded, investigators found that the business had been a pyramid scam.

In July 1983 the Alderdices were indicted on thirty-four counts of grand larceny and securities fraud in Florida federal court and on 200 counts of fraud by Broward County. While in the Metropolitan Correctional Institute in Dade County, James and William made the acquaintance of

James Doyle, also an inmate at the time. After they were released on bond, they maintained a friendship with Doyle. It was this "friend" who stabbed William Alderdice to death a year later, wounding James when he tried to intervene, reportedly in an argument over the use of William's car.

The $10 million owed to some 25,000 IGBE investors will probably never be recovered. When investigators checked the Alderdice vault, they found only an adding machine and forty ingots, which turned out to be blocks of wood painted gold. The brothers were notorious for high living, driving big cars, and taking Lear jets to the West Coast on a whim. It seems hard to believe that even the most dedicated fast-lane lifestyle enthusiasts could squander so much so quickly. Perhaps some of it is in a Cayman bank. Maybe it went to organized crime. We will probably never know.

6.

Trust Me, Baby: Bunco Romance

The marriage bunco artist is one of the strange ones. He'll never tell you the truth about himself because he doesn't know it himself. He goes through life making out on marriage bunco ... but he just thinks he's Lothario or someone and takes the ladies as they fall.

Anonymous con artist
Richard H. Blum, *Deceivers and Deceived*

The con artist who practices marriage and romance (M&R) bunco makes a living by fleecing the opposite sex. Great charm and seductiveness are required in this line of work; so is a cold heart. The con artist attracts the mark, quickly establishes intimacy, and creates an illusory love affair, all usually in less than a month's time. The mark is head over heels in love, but the con artist must remain uninvolved. He acts out the grand passion of a lifetime over and over again, each time with a different lover. He leaves behind a string of broken hearts and depleted bank accounts.

SWEETHEART SCAMS

Back in Mesquite, Texas, two-time world champion rodeo

cowboy Monty Henson was getting a mite nervous. Saddle-bronc champ in both 1975 and 1976, Henson was unfazed by bucking broncos and raging Brahman bulls, but tearful women distressed him. Especially when they were calling from several states at all hours to accuse him of dastardly deeds he hadn't even committed. Henson was therefore relieved when Terry Matlock, his self-styled double, was arrested and the troubles began to subside.

Matlock was practicing romance bunco with a twist—he added impersonation to his bag of tricks, availing himself of a ready-made reputation. Although the resemblance between Matlock and Henson was not great, Matlock cashed in on Henson's glamor and good name for a period of six months or more, romancing young women and liberating their money, valuables, and cars. Motel owners were conned by Matlock as well. As he left the premises, his latest pigeon on his arm, he would stop at the front desk to pay the bill with a phony credit card or forged check, or would charge his tab to the Professional Rodeo Cowboys' Association (PRCA).

One of the women duped by Matlock met the ersatz cow-poke in the little cafe in Pearl, Oklahoma, where she worked as a waitress. Young, attractive, and vulnerable—and impressed by rodeo stars—she fit the description of a typical Matlock victim. Posing as Monty Henson, he told her that he thought she was great, and that if she would fly to Denver, Colorado, he would take her on the rodeo circuit with him. Love at first sight! The waitress agreed.

Matlock is believed to have then stolen a car from another young woman and driven to Colorado. He picked up the waitress at Stapleton Airport in a chauffeured limousine. After stopping at the Marriott Hotel, they went on to Vail. Back at the Marriott, Matlock generously paid the driver with a counter check drawn on the Citizen's State Bank of Morland, Kansas, for $1,100. He signed the check *Monty Henson.*

One wild and wonderful weekend with the same waitress

was apparently enough for Matlock. Monday morning she awoke to find her honey had vamoosed with her money, and promptly went into hysterics. She called the police, and the desk called the Professional Rodeo Cowboys' Association, as Matlock had charged his stay to this organization. The PRCA headquarters in Colorado Springs gallantly bought the little lady a return ticket, and she went back to Pearl, a sadder but wiser woman (or so we assume).

As often happens, Matlock's arrest came about more by coincidence than as a result of the concerted efforts of law-enforcement officials to nab him. At a bar in Ten Sleep, Wyoming, he was grandstanding, pretending, as usual, to be Monty Henson. This time, however, a friend of Henson's happened to be within earshot. He quietly called the police, and Matlock was arrested for possession of a stolen credit card. Police routinely entered information about the arrest into a national law-enforcement computer, and soon requests to hold the prisoner were coming in from all over. Matlock was wanted in Alabama, Colorado, Florida, Kansas, Louisiana, Mississippi, Oklahoma, and Texas for impersonation, forgery, automobile theft, and defrauding an innkeeper.

Terry Matlock was practicing a type of romance bunco. The possibilities for scams in this confidence field are many and diverse. The con artist who specializes in marriage and romance is sometimes called a *sweetheart scammer*, or, if he is a man, a *mack*. He or she, even more than other con artists, is likely to have difficulty perceiving the line between reality and make-believe. Motivations are the same as those of other con men: a desire for profit and power over others. The M&R con is likely to have it in for the opposite sex and to enjoy getting revenge by means of bunco tactics. This is not easy for marks to pick up at first because no one is more charming than the professional love profiteer in action.

For the mack, bunco love has a definite advantage over real love, which would require that he be vulnerable. In the process of the con game, he is able to receive the affection and admiration of his mark without losing control over the situation and can thus manipulate his "lover" as a puppeteer works a marionette. The accomplished M&R artist knows just which strings to pull to get the desired reaction and enjoys playing cat and mouse with his victim.

For the victim, bunco love may seem better than the real thing, just as an airbrushed centerfold model in a glossy girlie magazine looks better than a flesh-and-blood lover. Professional packaging is the key to this seeming perfection, and the M&R artist tries hard to simulate the mark's ideal. The mark is only too happy to add to the illusion, and, in his or her desire for "true love," obligingly overlooks imperfections which might serve as clues to the heartthrob's true nature. Love, after all, like self-interest, is blind! Unfortunately, falling for a bunco artist is ultimately just as unfulfilling and a great deal more costly than falling for a centerfold.

Chris, a self-styled jack of all trades who prefers to make his living by confidence games, exemplifies the typical M&R artist, although he has never gone so far as to propose marriage to a mark. He specializes in short cons. He doesn't make much money from most of his exploits, but it's worth it to Chris just to victimize the women who fall for him.

"My goal is to get revenge on women," Chris stated in an interview. "I'm a good-looking guy, and I can talk to women. I know what to say. Also, you have to know how to pick them. In a meat market [singles bar], they're easy to spot. Girls that come in by themselves or with girlfriends, they're looking for something. They look around in a certain way. You have to recognize the body language. I also like to read the want ads, even notices on bulletin boards. I'm always on the lookout for these—when I go to the Laundromat or to university buildings—wherever I happen to be. A woman who's trying to sell something, or who needs a ride, or whatever—she's vulnerable. She's willing to be more open, because she really needs something. Usually you can get her to go to bed with you, loan you money, just about anything, as long as you act nice and polite and let her think you're in some kind of trouble. But she has to believe you're basically a nice guy, your intentions are honorable, and that soon she's going to get what she wants from you. That's not hard; most of them are suckers. If they've got a boyfriend lurking around, then I won't bother, 'cause the boyfriend can smell it.

"I get money. Twenty, thirty, sometimes fifty dollars. Usually you have to hang around longer to get more, and I'm not into that. . . . What I like best, though, is to call up after, and just listen to what she says, imagining the look on her face when she knows she's been screwed. There's nothing they can do, at that point. It makes my day."

Oddly enough, Chris's victims never catch on until after he has spelled it all out. Women seem to like and trust him, thinking that he is a great guy until after the fact. To date, he has never been reported to the police. So much for women's intuition. Perhaps someday one of those lurking boyfriends will give Chris his comeuppance.

MARRIAGE BUNCO

The marriage bunco specialist proposes matrimony as a means of loosening up his or her victim's purse strings. He hopes the mark will follow the old "what's mine is yours" philosophy once marriage is proposed. The con artist likes this philosophy, interpreting it to mean "what's yours is mine," and may stop just short of the altar or actually go through with the ceremony before absconding with the victim's money or possessions.

Some Previous Existence

Jody (she prefers that her last name be withheld), a real

estate saleswoman in Boulder, Colorado, suspected that her boyfriend Bill was a bit of a freeloader, but she was ready to put up with that. She was amazed when she discovered that he was a bigamist and flimflam man as well.

Jody tells her story:

He came into the office by himself, and I just happened to be the only one there. Said he was interested in buying some property for investment purposes. I drove him around. He seemed like the real thing, you know, rich, well-dressed, perfect manners. Except I guess he did ask me a lot of personal questions, and I might have been offended if he wasn't so good-looking. But then, he had such a nice smile. Friendly. And like he'd known me for a long time. Like he could kind of see into me . . . and he kidded me a lot, in a nice way, the way people'll kid a little girl. So I guess I confided in him quite a bit. . . . We had all these little personal jokes. I mean, almost right away. He said we'd met in some previous existence.

That's just how he put it: "Some previous existence." We started seeing each other. He found out what I liked best; then he bought me special things that no one else ever bothered with. Daffodils. My favorite kind of cookie. An album I wanted. He was so thoughtful sometimes.

There were other times, like when he went out with another woman and someone from the office told me. He had said he had to visit his grandmother. I just got so depressed. When I confronted him with it, he said, "Oh, honey, don't be mad. That girl is just a good friend, like a sister." I said to him, "Bill, what do you take me for?" And I guess the answer to that question is one thousand, one hundred ninety-seven dollars and eighty-five cents.

That's how much he got from me, not counting food or presents or booze. I know right down to the penny because that's how much I had in my savings account—the first money I'd been able to save in years.

But he was going to pay me back, he said. At the time I didn't feel there was any risk. He'd just moved here, and all his cash was tied up in Florida, but it wouldn't be long before he'd be rolling in dough. Then we were going to get married. It sounded great. Except for a couple of things that did kind of worry me.

Especially that he went out with that other woman. But, of course, he and I had only known each other four or five days then. It wasn't like we were engaged. But things went so fast, it seemed as if we'd always been in love. His dating other people just didn't fit in with what he was telling me. I wasn't going to say anything else, but then I did, and I cried. And then *he* cried. He said he was falling for me so fast that he was scared. That was why he went out with someone else—for ballast—only it didn't work. Nothing would, he said, except to marry me. And we were both crying, holding on to each other. I now realize it was all bull.

Did I mention that he was also great in bed? I thought it was something spiritual. He was always wanting to know what I wanted, what I liked. I don't like talking about it now, because at the time it seemed so special; it's hard for me to have to realize that he did the same thing with a lot of other women. And probably told each and every one of them that it was so good because they'd known each other in some previous existence. That kills me.

So, anyway, he had me coming and going. I withdrew that money from savings and handed it to him, temporarily, as I thought at the time, and never gave it so much as a second thought till much later. That money seemed unimportant to me, compared with my other concerns. I was seriously considering marrying Bill. And at this time we hadn't even known each other two weeks yet.

Then one day I was sitting in the office, thinking to myself, yes, I believe I will do it. I'll marry that man. And right at that moment, I'll swear, is when Lorna waltzed in. That girl has a sense of timing.

To make a long story short, Lorna told me that Bill was married to at least three women that she knew of, including herself, and proceeded to pull their pictures out of her wallet. One was cute, in sort of a high-school, cheerleader way. The other was an old bag. Lorna was sort of a bleached-blonde type, but not too bad.

So there I was, looking at these pictures—one of the women had a little boy that looked exactly like Bill— and feeling like if I stood up or tried to do anything too fast, I'd faint. It was unbelievable, and still I knew that Lorna was telling the truth.

She'd hunted me down, like she'd hunted down the other women. She'd been on Bill's trail for three years. Lorna wanted me to help her prosecute him, and I was going to do it, but in the end I couldn't.

I rehearsed this long speech I'd give to Bill. But when I saw him back at the apartment, the words didn't seem true anymore, and I couldn't talk. I started to bawl and told him about Lorna, and he was out of there, believe me. In thirty seconds flat, that man was history. That was eight and a half months ago, and I haven't heard from him since.

And you know what? It's funny. I believe he loves me. In his own way. Even though I know better, in part of my brain I still consider Bill to be the love of my life. Oh, sure, I see through that previous existence stuff, but sometimes it seems more real than anything that is currently happening in my life.

If he were to walk through that door right this minute, I don't think I'd fall for a word he'd say. But then, I really don't know.

Like any victim of bunco romance, Jody thinks of her affair with Bill as a unique experience. In fact, it is hard to imagine that thousands of women in the United States are hoodwinked by similar tricks every year. Police frequently do not act on similar cases when they are reported, in the mistaken belief that to do so would be to interfere in a domestic dispute or lovers' quarrel. Sophisticated bunco squads in big cities like Los Angeles, New York, and Washington, D.C., however, are familiar with romance and marriage scams and know that the con artists who routinely victimize women in this way follow certain recognizable operational patterns. The case of Giovanni Vigliotto [described below], known as "the man with 105 wives," while an extreme example, is in many respects typical marriage bunco.

A Marrying Fool

> *Heaven has no rage like love to hatred turned,*
> *Nor hell a fury like a woman scorned.*
> William Congreve, *The Mourning Bride*

> *My motto is, "Do whatever you want to me, but the payback's a bitch."*
> Sharon Clark Vigliotto

Sharon Clark was a little reluctant to marry the mysterious stranger who was whispering sweet nothings into her ear in seven languages. Giovanni Vigliotto, about fifty years of age, was exciting, personable, popular, and, by his own account, well-to-do. But Sharon Clark had already been married and divorced three times, and she wasn't sure whether she should make Giovanni number four. She had no way of knowing, of course, that although her lover had never been divorced, she would be wife number 104 in his book. Neither did she know that she was just Giovanni's type: a lonely, middle-aged woman with assets easily liquidated and funneled into his pocket.

Sharon, a flea-market manager, considered Giovanni loud and rude when she first met him in March 1981. He drove up in a white Cadillac to rent a booth, claiming to have $50,000 worth of merchandise to sell, wearing fancy cowboy clothes and sporting gold bracelets and a gold necklace from which hung gold toothpicks. She turned him down the first time he proposed. Over the course of two months, he wore down her resolve. He softened her heart by weeping as he recounted horror stories of how he had been made to watch as the Nazis raped and murdered his mother and sisters in Sicily. A gift of eight dozen yellow roses taped to two cases of Miller Lite beer didn't hurt his suit either. On a trip to Tennessee, Vigliotto and Clark were married by an old preacher in bib overalls, with barefoot Sharon dodging the chicken droppings that littered the yard around the preacher's shack. All in all, a romantic interlude, but the honeymoon was destined to be short-lived.

Giovanni convinced Sharon that they could make out like bandits by opening an antique shop in Texas. In June 1981, they loaded her antiques into her van and headed down to Florida to visit Sharon's mother, where Giovanni talked the elderly woman into moving to Texas with them. At his urging, she sold her retirement property for only $4,000; he told the women that they would have "lots of houses" in Texas. She allowed her son-in-law to take the proceeds for safekeeping, along with her valuables. That way, he said, everything would be ready for her when she arrived in Texas.

Claiming that he had business to take care of in Ohio, Giovanni drove the van to Dayton, where he left Sharon with $80, an old Jeep, and instructions to meet him in Detroit. When she arrived in Detroit, she found instructions to drive to a meeting place in Ontario. But in Canada there was no sign of her husband. Sharon got the picture.

She contacted a young flea marketer named John Boslett whom her fly-by-night husband had burned in Florida. Boslett got some money together and hitchhiked up to meet her; in October they set off together in pursuit of Mr. Wrong. The two had few clues aside from a road atlas in which Giovanni had circled likely flea-market towns, yet they tracked their quarry from Indiana to Arkansas to Texas to Mississippi to Florida. Sharon knew that they were on the right track when she spotted her belongings for sale in flea markets along the way. Three months later, with only three dollars between them, the dogged duo sighted the van in a parking lot in Panama City. Sharon was all for beating up her husband then and there, but John urged discretion, on the grounds that Giovanni might be armed. Remembering that he slept with a snub-nosed revolver on his pillow, Sharon contented herself with slashing the tires on the van and calling the police.

Giovanni, obviously a marrying kind of guy, had already wedded and defrauded wife number 105 in the six months that had elapsed since he abandoned Sharon in Ohio. His career seemingly at an end, he related many interesting stories about his past in the courtroom, although authorities have never been able to separate fact from fiction.

Giovanni Vigliotto has lived under perhaps 150 aliases. He says that his real name is Nikolai Peruskov and that he was born in Sicily and orphaned during World War II. (His given

name has not been documented, and the concensus is that he
cannot remember it himself.) According to his account, he
worked for the CIA during the 1950s and claimed it was the
CIA that brought him to the United States. He admitted to
marrying repeatedly without benefit of interceding divorce,
but tearfully denied swindling any of the 105 wives whose
names he was able to remember and list.

The prosecution told a different story, assembling a group
of wronged wives to testify against Giovanni. Earlier, when
these women had complained to police, they were told to
hire lawyers to settle their "matrimonial disputes." Until this
point they had been spouses with axes to grind rather than
fraud victims in the eyes of the law. According to the testimony of Deputy U.S. Marshal William Harrison, the defendant enjoyed writing to the women he had conned to let
them know what he had taken them for. "It was a game to
him," Harrison said.

Giovanni was emotional during the trial. He wept frequently, raged, and attempted to slam out of the courtroom.
He fired and rehired his public defender. Certainly, confronted with all those wives, he had reason to feel edgy. The
jury of eight men and four women were unswayed by his his-
trionics. In February 1983, he was convicted of bigamy and
defrauding wife 105, Patricia Ann Gardner, and was sentenced to thirty-four years in prison.

It is an interesting comment on the character of Sharon
Clark that she entertained no more sympathy for the other
women cheated by Giovanni than for Giovanni himself. In
an interview with *People* magazine, Sharon declared: "I
figure 90 percent of them deserved it. I deserved it, too,
because I was so gullible, but I'm different from most
women. Some of them should have gone out, dammit, and
done something."

The "Crayfish"

Not all M&R bunco artists are men. Women have shown

quite an aptitude for sweetheart hustles in their own right. A friend from Wisconsin told me about a relationship between his grandfather and a nurse that had the look of bunco, although no charges were filed, and probably no fraud could have been proven in any case.

My friend's grandparents—I'll call them Mr. and Mrs. Morganthal—had been married for upwards of fifty years, and by all accounts had always been a reasonably happy couple. The trouble began when they hired a part-time nurse.

Both Mr. and Mrs. Morganthal were feeling crochety and not at all well. Mrs. M had taken to her bed after a stroke, and the family feared that she would never get out of it again. Mr. M had a bad heart. He also had plenty of money and a fine home where he preferred to remain rather than move to some smaller, "convenient" apartment in an establishment for the elderly. An institution was out of the question. To stay in their own home, however, the couple required a nurse to help out. And that's where Dorothy Cray came in.

My friend met Miss Cray, whom he referred to as the *Crayfish*, and was not impressed with her looks. His grandfather, on the other hand, was taken with her from the start. Although Mr. M called her "that young girl," the Crayfish was thirty-two at the time she was hired. She had red hair and a way of giggling like a schoolgirl, at least during the early days of her employ. Mr. M quickly fell in love with her, my friend says.

The old gentleman maddened his family by insisting that "that young girl, Dot" was entirely devoted to him, in a way that Mrs. M had never been. Perversely, the nurse did at first work wonders for the couple's health. Mr. M was now spry and twinkling, while Mrs. M grimly improved as she saw what was going on between her husband and the young adventuress. It was as if she forced herself to get better so that she could put a stop to his foolishness.

Both Mr. and Mrs. M were especially fond of their great-grandson, a little boy named Peter. Crayfish likewise made a big fuss over the child when he came to visit, talking to him via "Baa" the lamb, a fluffy puppet she had bought especially for this purpose. She was motherly with little Peter and equally solicitous of Mr. M, constantly urging him to wear his sweater and straightening his lap robe for him. Mrs. M rebuffed what few services were offered her, waving Crayfish away and managing for herself. She dismissed Crayfish several times, but Mr. M always reinstated her.

This went on for two or three months. The family now refused to visit during the Crayfish's working hours, and began to offer Mrs. M their spare bedrooms. She refused their invitations.

"I am the lady of this house," she would state, "and here I'll stay." A weaker woman might have given in and allowed the apparent hussy to drive her out, but Mrs. M remained, growing stubbornly fitter every day. Still, she lost her battle with the Crayfish.

The younger woman, seeing that Mrs. M was not going to die as soon as she had expected, convinced Mr. M to sue for divorce. He broke the news to Mrs. M, whereupon she had another stroke, this time a fatal one. From what I hear, Crayfish showed herself to be indecently happy at the funeral. She promptly resigned her position as nurse, trading her white uniform for pastel dresses, big straw hats, and high heels. No attempt was made to explain her presence in the house after she had given notice.

Her happiness was no doubt attributable to the fact that now, with no divorce to divide the Morganthal estate, she would gain control of the entire fortune. Very soon she herself became Mrs. M, coincident with which event her fondness for little Peter abruptly vanished. Baa disappeared into a drawer, never to be seen again. She also seemed to lose her interest in straightening Mr. M's lap robe and coaxing him into his sweater. Mr. M noticed the change but attributed it to her grief at losing her employer, the original Mrs. M.

"Dot's a loyal young girl," he would declare, "no matter what Lettie used to say about her, and no one is more upset about Lettie's passing than young Dot here." At these words, the Crayfish would sneer, and the family members would steam. Mr. M kept up this tack until he died during one of his afternoon naps.

The Crayfish inherited the entire Morganthal estate. None of the family, including the great-grandson, got a cent, though the will is being contested. So Dorothy Cray made several million dollars in less than six months' time. Not bad for a part-time nurse. She still lives in the mansion, which has been in the family for generations. The other Morganthals who live in town drive out of their way to spare themselves the sight of the Crayfish, kneeling beside the pink flamingos that now adorn the front yard, spading the pansy garden in her mink coat.

SIGHT-UNSEEN ROMANCE BUNCO

Lonely hearts clubs have traditionally been rich sources of victims for con artists and gold diggers of all kinds. Nowadays emotionally needy souls can readily be located through personals columns and computer-dating services as well. Some of the people who seek human contact through such channels are lonely enough that they can be victimized long distance, without ever meeting their sweethearts face-to-face. Various pen pal scams, for example, have been practiced for generations, whereby "mail-order brides" are sent generous amounts of traveling money by hopeful prospective bridegrooms. The love letters cease and the "bride's" train never arrives at the station.

The story of Ron Reed is an example of a sight-unseen romance bunco scam. Bizarre as it sounds, his case is not unusual. Ron arrived in Toledo, Ohio, in 1970, a friendless, twenty-eight-year-old in need of companionship. In the frame of mind he was in, he felt open to just about anything that might steer him in the direction of a more fulfilling life, including the advice of a fortune-teller. He heard of an astrologer who was practicing in town and decided to consult her. It was his bad fortune that the astrologer happened to be a young woman named Carolyn Matuszak.

Matuszak didn't have to be psychic to see that Ron Reed was lonely and therefore suggestible. After assuring him that his horoscope showed that love was just around the corner, she casually informed him that her best friend was lonely, too.

Matuszak described this friend as a beautiful, blond young woman named Kyle Stratton who stood to inherit a large fortune. Her loneliness was due to a car accident which had left her isolated in a hospital room where she was hooked up to a dialysis machine. A hard-hearted lawyer in a distant city was in charge of her affairs and had contrived to have the hospital forbid all visitors except for Carolyn Matuszak.

When Ron expressed sympathy for the young patient, Matuszak suggested that he correspond with her as a pen pal. It would do both of them good, she said. Ron should write to Kyle right away; Matuszak would smuggle their letters in and out of the hospital. Ron agreed to such an arrangement.

With Matuszak acting as confidante, a romance grew between the bedridden heiress and the lonely man. Kyle sent photographs, which revealed that she was indeed beautiful, along with friendly, warm messages. Later Kyle was able to telephone Ron on the sly, and her voice and personality completely won him over. After a while, Matuszak mentioned that, while Kyle herself would never complain, she was having a bad time of it with her lawyer. He was restricting the amount of money she could divert from her estate to a trickle, so that she was deprived not only of the small luxuries that made her confined life bearable, but of the dialysis required to keep her kidneys functioning properly.

When Ron began sending money and gifts, Kyle's phone conversations and letters became even warmer. Friendship turned to passion as more and more money and presents were delivered through Matuszak. On three occasions, when Kyle needed operations or special care, Ron took out loans to cover expenses. He told Kyle everything, and she in turn listened and lent support. Daily letters and frequent photographs of Kyle kept Ron going.

This went on for years—ten years, in fact. Kyle had begun calling Ron her husband, and he had begun to think of himself as married. He didn't go out with anyone, feeling that to do so would be unfaithful to Kyle. When he began cutting back on the money he sent to her in order to make payments for a new car, Matuszak became incensed. His loyalties should be to his wife, she told Ron indignantly, and not to some automobile dealer. Which was more important, Kyle or a new car?

This shook Ron up pretty badly. Feeling guilty and confused, he spilled out his story to a friend. The friend thought the whole thing sounded fishy and sent Ron to the police. The police began an investigation.

It wasn't easy for the detective in charge of the case to report the findings to Ron. He felt sorry for Ron, who, he said, had trouble believing that Kyle was no more than a fictitious character invented and played by Carolyn Matuszak. After all, he had loved Kyle for ten years. Now, suddenly, he had nothing; his life had lost its focus. The police referred to Ron's ten-year devotion to Kyle as "a thing of beauty."

And, as if it weren't bad enough to have been in love with an illusion for a decade, this fantasy woman had not even been exclusively his own: Kyle had managed to lead a secret life during the time she was "married" to Ron. At least twenty other people had been corresponding with her, sending letters, gifts, flowers, and money through the astrologer go-between, Matuszak. One man had sent $6,000 worth of roses in two years.

Ron did find a real woman, though, to replace the shadow he had loved for so long. According to Ron, she was understanding, real, and embraceable. He felt that his wife had died but that he had to go on. It was, he said, what Kyle would have wanted.

Although Ron lost $10,000 through the hoax (Matuszak repaid $30,000 of the $40,000 Ron had spent on Kyle), he refused to press charges. None of "Kyle's" other friends, well-wishers, and "husbands" pressed charges either.

PREVENTION: THE BEST CURE

Marius said, "I see the cure is not worth the pain."
Plutarch, *Lives, Caius Marius*

I could've had the jerk skip-traced, but it wasn't worth the aggravation.
Anonymous marriage-swindle victim

Revenge may be sweet, but, by the time the romance roller-coaster ride is over, most M&R victims have little stomach for it. The Sharon Clarks of this world are one in a hundred. Or, to be exact, one in one-hundred five. According to Dan Eisenberg, president of Tracers Company of America, people who have been taken in by a con artist often refuse to follow through or prosecute because they don't want to get reinvolved with the culprit. Reluctant to reopen a painful wound or to rock the boat, they usually let the matter drop and rationalize the swindle as best they can.

Eisenberg has worked for Tracers since 1958, and knows whereof he speaks when he discourses on swindlers and the swindled. His New York City P.I. firm, established in 1924, specializes in all aspects of background investigation. Its investigators will also track missing persons; over the years Tracers has located over ten thousand M&R bunco artists for clients and have helped many to retrieve money and valuables.

Today, Eisenberg says, requests for such services have fallen off. In the past, women who felt embarrassed for falling for such cons relied on the discretion of Tracers. "They wanted things hush-hush." Now women are less embarrassed, but more apt to "take it on the chin."

In a con situation, Eisenberg believes, the victim may be either *uninitiated*—naive—or a sophisticated person who enjoys something about the relationship he has with the con artist. The latter type is frequently a *repeater*, someone who falls for a con even when he knows better.

When the stakes are high in a budding romance or a business situation and there is room for doubt, Eisenberg advises a good P.I. firm be consulted before involvement becomes too deep. Too many people will take a third party's word when that person doesn't have all the facts at his disposal. "They ask their brother-in-law. He doesn't know what he's talking about, but he doesn't like to admit it," says Eisenberg. A background investigation, discreetly handled, can save a lot of grief.

One wealthy woman, for example, had doubts about her fiancé and hired Tracers to check him out. Investigators discovered that her intended was using an alias to impersonate an M.D., was previously married, had been arrested for impersonating an officer, and had served a prison term for swindling women.

What if a person suspects bunco, but has neither the funds nor the desire to hire a P.I.? Eisenberg says that tracing a missing person is largely a matter of using logic, but that it is better to be careful in the first place. If one could be "always a skeptic," he or she would generally avoid being duped. When a prospective lover seems too good to be true, you have to be careful. But, he adds, many times we purposely look the other way because there is something in the relationship we like. This can be all right, too, but you have to know where to draw the line. You can enjoy a physical relationship, for instance, without ladling out money or getting married. And, unless you get a thrill out of being taken for a ride, check out the facts in a logical way when you sense that something is amiss. It's up to you to decide when to bail out.

7.

Spiritual Bunco

There are more things in heaven and earth, Horatio,
Than are dreamt of in your philosophy.
                    Shakespeare, *Hamlet,* I, *v*, 166

At the outset of this chapter it must be emphasized that, as neither the author nor the editor has any claim to absolute knowledge of the cosmos, no attempt will be made herein to devalue the belief of any individual, or to criticize his search for the Truth, or any truth. The purpose of the chapter is solely to point out the con artist's cynical abuse of the faith of others.

Twentieth-Century Spiritualism

On the current world scene, belief in the paranormal is fed and reinforced by a vast media industry that profits from it, and it has been transformed into a folk religion, perhaps the dominant one today.

Paul Kurtz
Founder of the Committee for the Scientific
Investigation of Claims of the Paranormal

It has become apparent that the twentieth century, known as the Age of Technology, has another face as well. Mankind's quest for the spiritual has not been annihilated by scientific rationalism. During the Seventies, Eastern religions and such cults as the Moonies and Scientology came into their own in the United States, winning thousands of converts among white-collar, urban young people. In the Eighties, fundamentalist, charismatic, and deliverance Christian sects have moved from the farm to the city to be embraced by educated and uneducated folks across the country.

And it isn't just religion that people are turning to in their hunger for the spiritual. All kinds of superstitions have gained popularity and even public acceptance in recent years; take, for example, the current interest in astrology, witchcraft, UFOs, the Bermuda Triangle, and biorhythms. For whatever reason, many Americans want to place themselves in the hands of a higher power, and in such a way that they will not be required to think or act for themselves. They prefer to believe that their lives depend more upon Divine Will, Fate, or the Stars than on their own actions.

What all of this means for the con artist is a permanent address on Easy Street. If he is a charismatic person (as many con artists are) and sufficiently unscrupulous, he has only to find himself the right niche in the spiritual scene and he can put anything over on his faithful following.

Desperate people turn to the supernatural after other avenues have failed. They come seeking The Answer, wanting to believe. The spiritual bunco artist is waiting for them with open arms, and he does not disappoint them. Or at least not at this stage of the game. He is perfectly willing to pretend that he has The Answer, whether he is a pastor or an astrologer. His quest is for power and money, and he makes out with the flock like a wolf in sheep's clothing.

His authority is now beyond mere mortal comprehension. He's got a hot line to God, or to the realm of departed spirits, or even to an ambassador from another galaxy. So who are you to question him?

MAN OF THE CLOTH

For the love of money is the root of all evil: which while some coveted after, they have erred from the faith, and pierced themselves through with many sorrows.

I Timothy I.10

The Devil can quote scripture.

American proverb

The Christian church has a long tradition of men and women, devoted to God and their fellowman, who have worked selflessly for good. It has an equally long tradition of scammers devoted to their own self-interest, who have worked selfishly for their own good. A con artist in the church can spout scripture with the best of them, and twist it around to suit his purposes. He can act smug and sanctimonious while diverting church funds to his own pocket.

Where religions and financial business mix, the opportunity for fraud increases. The Baptist Foundation of America scandal is one case in which ministers traded on their unblemished reputations to lend respectability to less-than-honorable financial dealings. The Foundation issued $26 million in notes to the public in order to acquire subsidiaries. The notes were worthless, but this was not discovered until after they had been accepted by many highly respected lending institutions. Donations of assets, appraised at far more than their value, were accepted by the Foundation in order to allow the donors to take huge tax deductions.

Charles E. Blair, pastor of the six-thousand-member Calvary Temple in Denver, was involved in a similar enterprise. He was televising sermons to eleven states, traveling across the country and to Europe to speak to large audiences, and expanding his own church when his financial empire collapsed in 1976. He declared his three foundations (Life Center, The Charles E. Blair Foundation, and Calvary Temple) bankrupt, leaving 3,400 investors out $12 million. Blair was convicted on seventeen counts of securities fraud, given five years' probation, fined $5,000, and ordered to repay investors.

According to Blair, it was God's will that he expand his ministry. To do so, he purchased Life Center, a Denver nursing home, financing the expenditure by selling securities in the name of the three foundations.

Blair's wife, Betty, never believed that he was guilty of fraud. "He's always had the goodness of people at heart," stated Mrs. Blair. "We are both children of the Depression and had a drive to do something important, to be successful."

Blair's congregation obviously agreed. Calvary Temple still had a membership of six thousand after the pastor's conviction, and he continued to broadcast his teachings to eleven states every Sunday morning. Whatever Blair's intentions may have been, the example stands as an illustration of how a church can be used for less than holy purposes.

Another type of financial con perpetrated under church auspices was reported by the nephew of a storefront church minister who preferred that no names be published in the account. While to his knowledge most storefront churches are operated legitimately, he said, his uncle (we'll call him Father L) strayed from the straight and narrow.

Father L's favorite scam was Gambling Night, a monthly extravaganza he initiated soon after he set up his storefront ministry. He had left his ministry at a larger church because of differences with some of its high-ranking members and needed cash badly. Gambling Night did the trick for him. Whereas church attendance at the storefront church was maybe thirty-five people on Christmas and Easter, half the town would turn out for his money-making bashes. Bingo, card games, roulette, and dicing were practiced. Although gambling was illegal, the police never interfered. Father L played his part well, radiating brotherly love and authority, and no one liked to question him, least of all when they were winning. On a good night he collected as much as $10,000 and kept it as part of his salary for doing the Lord's work. Naturally, he paid no taxes on his take.

Another source of tax-free income for Father L was real estate. He bought, sold, and rented property, always at a profit, leaving the properties in the church's name. This would have been legitimate, except that he diverted most of the money into his bank account.

Whether Father L's conscience troubled him is anybody's guess, but his nephew said that family members sometimes heard him shouting at Satan in his sleep. He always maintained an air of respectability, and in his sermons he denounced every sort of dishonesty practiced by others. His righteous manner was believable enough that when he died his congregation praised him as an inspiration to do good works.

While there are doubtless accomplished con artists among the charismatic leaders of some Christian sects as well as other religious groups, they are difficult to identify unless they are caught in financial scams. Even then, there is frequently controversy over First Amendment rights. There will never be widespread agreement when it comes to separating the rogues from the enlightened (and there can even be such a thing as an enlightened rogue!). The danger of following a leader who possesses both charisma and criminal tendencies has been adequately sensationalized by the media coverage of such cult figures as Charles Manson and Jim Jones; there is no need to go into the subject here. The individual is on his own when it comes to making value judgments—let the seeker beware.

SPIRITUAL ADVISORS

While not all so-called spiritual advisors are con artists, care should be taken when consulting astrologers, palmists, tarot readers, and others who sell psychic services. The potential for chicanery in this field is enormous.

Gypsy Blessing

There are lies more believable than truth.
Gypsy saying
Jan Yoors, *The Gypsies*

A woman wrote recently to Dear Abby about her visits to a "spiritual reader" who claimed to have the power to see both the past and the future and to make wishes come true. The initial consultation fee was twenty dollars, which the woman paid. The fortune-teller then asked her for another twenty dollars for a candle. The candle would be burnt, the fortune-teller said, to bring back the woman's lost love. On her next appointment, the woman was told that evil spirits had blown out the first candle; the price for another would be fifty dollars. When the woman explained that she had no more money, the fortune-teller asked her to leave her VISA card so that something could be bought for the church. This would supposedly help to return the errant lover. The woman told Abby that she would do anything in order to get him back, but wondered whether this spiritual reader was on the up-and-up. (Abby told her to report the fraud to her local police department's bunco squad.)

Strange as it may seem, the story is an old one, and very common. Gypsy crime in the United States accounts for about $300 million in losses each year, according to *Centurion*, a police magazine. And fortune-telling is one of the major Gypsy crimes.

Police often do not know that they are dealing with Gypsies, and so many of these crimes are not reported as such, says Terry Getsay, a criminal intelligence analyst with the Illinois Department of Law Enforcement. Gypsies in the United States today cannot be distinguished by their clothing, although married women wear headscarves instead of wedding rings. Getsay states that Gypsies, when arrested, may claim to be American Indians or natives of other countries, although he has heard of cases in which Gypsies filed defamation suits against police departments and city governments because they were labled Yugoslavians or Bulgarians in police reports.

The word *gypsy* comes from *Egyptian*, probably because gypsies referred to themselves as "Lords of Egypt" when they migrated to Europe in the fourteenth or fifteenth century. A nomadic people, they originally came from the border region between Iran and India. Gypsies first arrived in the United States from Europe in 1715, but most came during World War II, fleeing Nazi exterminations as *Untermenschen* ("subhumans"). Our slang expression *to gyp,* meaning *to cheat,* is derived from the word *gypsy.*

This is not as slanderous as it may seem. Gypsies—or *the Rom,* as they call themselves—follow a moral code that distinguishes between stealing from their own people, which is taboo, and stealing from the *Gaje* (everyone else), which is necessary. The women are particularly skillful at thievery and confidence games, particularly fortune-telling. Many Gypsy fathers still exact a bride price for their daughters. Those young women who have proven themselves to be the best thieves bring the highest prices, sometimes amounting to as much as $15,000. While some psychics and fortune-tellers are sincere in their work, the Gypsy spiritualists are a cynical lot. They do not practice their occult arts on their own kind, but only on the Gaje, as a rip-off technique.

The "Gypsy Blessing" is a con game practiced by fortune-tellers on the unwary. In order for the game to work, the victim must be unhappy or in some kind of trouble, so that he or she is ready to believe just about anything the Gypsy says when she offers her "assistance." The Gypsy is not psychic, but generations of Romany mothers have passed down the tricks of the trade to their daughters, with the result that the Gypsy woman is a good amateur psychologist and an excellent con artist.

Nadine Pine, a sixty-five-year-old woman with a college education and a sizable bank account, visited a Gypsy fortune-teller with a friend. The two merely went on a whim the first time. They often had lunch together, and palm reading was advertised as an extra at a "fine tearoom" in Detroit. As Nadine Pine learned later, fortune-telling for money is illegal in Michigan, and the tearoom was merely a front. She and her friend each paid five dollars for a soggy sandwich, and then Madam Estelle came in.

The friend didn't think much of her reading, but with Nadine Pine it was different. She was still grieving over the death of her husband two years earlier, a fact that Madam Estelle was quick to divine with her well-used pack of tarot cards.

"Why is your wedding ring in your pocket?" inquired the fortune-teller. Amazed and embarrassed, Mrs. Pine removed it and pushed it back on her finger. This took some time, as her knuckle was swollen from forty years of wearing the wedding band, but it did not occur to her that this might provide a clue to an eye trained to notice such details.

Visits to Madam Estelle became frequent, as the Gypsy claimed to come closer and closer to getting in touch with Mr. Pine. Nadine Pine, like many widowed women, sometimes dreamed that she was talking to her husband, and the dreams were vivid. She wanted to believe that he was trying to communicate with her, and she particularly wanted to know whether she would see him again after her death. Eventually, Madam Estelle was able to get a few cryptic words out of Mr. Pine's spirit, but never quite enough to satisfy his wife. The messages only made her eager to hear more. And, of course, the soggy sandwiches were growing outrageously expensive.

When Nadine Pine's thirty-year-old son Roger returned from a two-year stint in Australia, his mother couldn't resist telling him about Madam Estelle's conversation with his dad. Roger was upset, both because he saw that his mother was being used and because she had spent the funds that she had promised to him and his wife as a down payment for a house. He contacted the police, who surprised Madam Estelle before she had a chance to relocate under an assumed name (her usual M.O.).

Roger was able to reason with his mother and convinced her to press charges against the fortune-teller. Madam Estelle was convicted of theft, put on three years' probation, and ordered to pay back the $30,000 she had conned from Nadine Pine.

Women are not the only victims of the Gypsy blessing. After his two Saint Bernards died mysteriously, Benjamin Shepherd, a fifty-seven-year-old electrician, grew depressed and began to believe that he was cursed by bad luck. He went to see Patricia and Tina Stevens, a mother-and-daughter team, who practiced fortune-telling in Camden County, New Jersey. Patricia and Tina agreed that Benjamin was under a curse but assured him that the bad luck could be removed. All he had to do was buy a chicken in an Italian market in Philadelphia and bring it to them. Oh, yes, and bring along your $116,000, too, they said. The money in his savings account was responsible for his trouble.

Shepherd had some doubts, which he related to law-enforcement officials. When he returned with the chicken and the cash, he was wired with a miniature tape recorder, courtesy of the local police department. The two women blindfolded him, telling him that they were burning his money and transferring the bad luck to the fowl, which they then killed.

The Stevens women were arrested and pleaded guilty to charges of fraud. They were ordered to return his money (which they had not burned, of course) and 10 percent interest.

Shepherd was still out one chicken, but he fared better than the large majority of Gypsy blessing victims. So did Nadine Pine. Most never recover their money. Many, on discovering that they have been swindled, are too ashamed to report the fraud to authorities, and those who do rarely see the culprit brought to trial.

Seeing Stars

Gypsies are not the only con artists who use the occult as a means of fleecing their marks. Every large city is teeming with mediums, astrologers, spiritual advisors, and what-have-you who will gladly tell you what you want to hear for a price. Some merely dally with the supernatural as a source of entertainment. Others truly believe in their psychic ability, and a few of these may indeed be gifted. Who knows? Even police departments sometimes call upon the aid of psychics when all else fails, although the good this has done is questionable. And, of course, there are always those who can't resist taking the suckers who come with money in hand for everything they can get.

A man I know told me that he used to call himself "Amazing Alvin" for business purposes. Perhaps his only gifts were a sympathetic face and a glib tongue, but they paid off for him when used in conjunction with a deck of tarot cards. This is amazing Alvin's story:

It was easy. The hardest part was familiarizing myself with the cards, learning various meanings and associations for each one. Lots of people thought they were skeptical, but the ones that said they were most skeptical usually told me the most about themselves and came to believe in what I was saying. I read people's cards at thirty bucks a hand for over a year—I used the Celtic Cross spread—and in all that time, no one ever told me I was wrong. Oh, well, sometimes they did, when I first did the reading, but then they'd come back and say they were really blown away, everything I told them came true. Usually it was pretty vague, but I was on target. What no one caught on to was that they'd *tell* me everything, while I acted like I was figuring out an obscure message in the cards, concentrating. I'd act like I didn't hear them. "Uh huh," I'd say, like they were interrupting my train of thought. People will confide anything while you're doing their spread.

And the cards did make patterns; I got so I half believed in it all myself. I ate it up when people told me how good I was, and I thought I was psychic. I still think I am intuitive, to a degree, but that's all.

Finally the whole scene started to sicken me. Here I was making all this money listening to people's troubles, and I was acting like a big guru, telling them what they should be doing with their lives. It got to be a power trip, and I got sick of myself. Now I can't even look at a tarot deck. People still ask me to do a reading for them every once in a while, but I'm not into it.

Tom Roper was not so lucky as to run into a con man with a conscience. Just out of college, he was at a turning point in his life when he contacted Timon, an astrologer in Boulder, Colorado. Timon was a believer himself; word had it that he slept with a ring of white quartz crystals around his bed to ward off evil spirits. He had bad nightmares, and he caused a few as well. Still, Timon wasn't so crazy that he couldn't do business with a clear head. One of his most useful confidence techniques was to frighten people so badly with his visions of their futures that they came to depend on him for advice and reassurance. Clients were constantly calling him, asking whether the signs were auspicious for buying a new car, going fishing, or interviewing for a job. Timon seemed to love the feeling of power he derived from his work, and he made a good living from it, too. He started off by charging reasonable fees for his forays into the future. Then, as a client's dependency increased, he would charge increasingly higher rates for his services. It *was* uncanny how often his predictions proved correct, although most were open to very broad interpretation.

At the time of Tom's astrological reading, it was obvious that he was confused and troubled, and Timon immediately picked up on Tom's emotional state. He said that Saturn had entered Tom's chart, where it was squared with Tom's sun in some house or other. Anyone who knew Tom could have told him that he was in a bad way, without consulting the stars or anything else. But, of course, nobody *would* tell him, except for Timon.

Timon confidently predicted that Tom would "lose it" within the next two months. While giving him this unpleasant news, he also fed Tom some crumbs of reassurance. When Tom lost it, Timon said he would be there to guide him, and to shield him from the malefic influences of the stars. At this meeting, he extracted sixteen dollars from Tom, the exact sum Tom had on him, and said that they could work out an equitable payment program for subsequent visits.

Not long afterward, Tom did lose it; he suffered a nervous breakdown. His behavior became extremely erratic, one moment belligerent, the next moment lethargic and depressed. Some people maintained that Timon had caused the breakdown by telling Tom that he would have one when he was obviously in an unstable and suggestible state. Others believed that Timon had predicted, not precipitated, the breakdown, and began referring their friends to him.

Whatever the case may have been, Timon never got more than sixteen dollars for his prediction, because for at least a year Tom couldn't keep an appointment. He didn't get up for work, stood up dates, and forgot to show up for his sister's wedding. He also broke every appointment Timon arranged after that first, momentous, visit.

The Seance

Con artists who specialize in spiritual bunco often rely on the seance as a means of separating victims from their money and possessions. The purpose of the seance—at least from the client's point of view—is to communicate with the spirits of people who have died. The psychic, or medium, is in charge of coaxing the spirits to speak. To this end, a number of people are gathered around a table in a partially darkened room; typically, there is a candle burning on the table. The participants hold hands, close their eyes, and direct their energies to invoking the departed soul, while the medium intones a litany of phrases calculated to break the spiritual ice. When the spirit consents to communicate, it is through the medium. The communication may take the form of speech, with the medium as mouthpiece; automatic writing, whereby the medium's hand is guided across the paper by an unseen force; rapping out *yes* and *no* or alphabetical messages (one rap for *A*, two raps for *B*, and so on); or a message spelled out on a Ouija board (unseen force guiding the hand again). Those who have participated in seances describe them as emotional, spooky, frightening, or religious experiences.

In Boston, during the autumn of 1976, Rosellen Blodgett was conned by a woman who held seances, and she hasn't been able to put the memory of that ordeal to rest yet.

"Tricking somebody in the way Mab tricked me is just so

low," she says. "If I could get ahold of her, I would make her tell me why she did it—and how she could have the heart to take advantage of a grieving person in that way."

Mab's real name, as police later informed Rosellen, was Joan Oderkirk. In her role as medium, however, she called herself Queen Mab, explaining that she had inherited her psychic powers from her Irish grandmother, who had been gifted with second sight when she was only five. Her basic method of operation was to advertise seances through leaflets left at supermarkets, Laundromats, and department-store rest rooms. When a prospective participant called, she would interview her privately, asking her reasons for wishing to communicate with the spirit world. This was a screening process, Queen Mab explained, to filter out those who had impure motives or who were mere sensation-seekers. To allow such people to take part in a seance would possibly break the magic circle, thus rendering communication impossible, or— far worse—invite malicious, evil spirits into the room. In reality, the interviews were used to discover other salient information, such as the mark's income, inheritance, and areas of vulnerability.

Rosellen was seeking her mother's forgiveness; she and her mother had always been very close until Rosellen decided to drop out of college and move in with a boyfriend of whom her family did not approve. Angry that her mother refused to accept her decision, Rosellen cut off all communication with her, and told no one in the family where she was living. Her mother died suddenly of an aneurysm; Rosellen found out about it two days afterward. She found it impossible to live with her guilt, and decided to try Queen Mab's seance as a means of making things right between her mother and herself. While she did not entirely believe that the seance would work, she was ready to try anything.

Looking back on her interview with Queen Mab, Rosellen

remembers that the medium appeared to be very sympathetic.

"Do you have anything very special that your mother gave you that we could use as a way to establish communication?" she asked, looking at Rosellen's hand. Rosellen was wearing a gold ring with a large red stone, and, yes, it had been a gift from her mother, passed down in the family for three generations. Queen Mab assured her the ring would be just the thing they needed.

At the seance, there were about ten people around the table, all women. The room was dim, lit only by three candles that sent shadows reeling along the walls and across the bowed faces of the participants. Rosellen remembered the candles because they were scented with an imitation floral scent she knew her mother would have hated. This was the first intimation she had that she should leave and not come back. Denying this impulse, she closed her eyes, bowed her head, and held hands with the women seated next to her.

For a long time, Queen Mab muttered and mumbled in a lulling singsong. Then her voice began to show excitement. The spirits were arriving!

The first spirit was that of an unborn child who could not sleep until he was given a name; Rosellen felt the pressure on her right hand increase, as her neighbor gasped. A lonely woman from Colonial days who had waited all her life for her fiancé to return home from the sea spoke next, and afterward came a string of messages from different spirits, all of them apparently trying to speak at once. Rosellen had never heard such intermittent whines, laughter, and angry exclamations from any one person's lips before!

Then it was her turn. Through Queen Mab, Rosellen's mother sweetly gave her assurance that all was forgiven, that there was nothing, in fact, to forgive. She asked only that

Rosellen take the ring she had left her and mail it to an address in Connecticut with no note of explanation. In her own youth, her mother said, she had a young, beloved friend who had died in childbirth. She now knew that the child born to her friend, just one year to the day older than Rosellen, was living in poverty and in need of help.

"But, mother," Rosellen blurted out at this point, "I had the ring appraised—just out of interest, I would never have sold it—and they told me it was valuable only for its sentiment. It's only worth about twenty dollars or so. Should I just send money instead?"

There was a little croaking sound, Rosellen remembers, then a pause. "Um, yes, that would be fine," Queen Mab said finally, and another spirit took the floor.

"Looking back," Rosellen now says, "it's obvious that it was a rip-off. I probably really knew at the time that the seance was a setup. But I needed that kind of absolution. I went home and put all the cash I could scrape together into an envelope and sent it to the address in Connecticut. It was several months later that I realized how close I came to giving away the one thing that really means a lot to me as a keepsake of my mom; it's a lot more important than the money. And that's what makes me so angry with that woman, that she would stoop so low as to prey on people in the condition I was in then."

Police were able to tell Rosellen that the medium had been a belly dancer, shoplifter, and check-forger at various stages in her career and that she had fleeced at least a dozen people in her seance scam. Most, the officer explained, probably had never complained, or, like Rosellen, had contacted the bunco squad too late. Joan Oderkirk, alias Queen Mab, is still at large.

A WORD TO THE WISE

One way to avoid getting ripped off by occultists is to

follow the advice an old Zen Buddhist monk gave to a woman who was fascinated with the paranormal. When she told him that she was catching glimpses of past and future lives, he listened attentively. When she asked whether he thought that such visions were possible, he nodded. When she asked what it all meant, he told her that it was none of her business.

In essence, he said that while there is much that is beyond our comprehension in the universe, it is best not to let the unknowable distract us from the job at hand, which is here and now. Live this life well, he said, and let the rest take care of itself.

8.

The Great Pyramid

Never give a sucker an even break.
Edward Francis Albee

In the business world, the greenback is king, and the fast-talking, quick-witted confidence artist is right in his element. To many an uptown grifter, the pyramid principle has been, and continues to be, a tremendous attraction.

The basis of all money-making pyramid schemes is the recruitment of new contributors rather than proper investment of funds or sales of goods and services. Each recruit must pay in a certain amount of money, which goes to those higher up in the "business" and to earlier investors. In order to recoup his cash outlay, a recruit must enlist several more contributors. The weakness inherent in any pyramid scheme is the numerical impossibility of recruiting ever-increasing numbers of contributors. Those at the bottom of the pyramid pay for those at the top, and only the originators of the scheme and the initial contributors, now at the peak of the pyramid, make a profit. It has been calculated that fewer than one-tenth of the participants stand to receive a worthwhile return, while more than half can expect to kiss their entire investment good-bye.

The cagey fellow who is running the scam will, of course,

tell you otherwise. He will try to generate enough excitement with inflated promises of vast profits to blind you to the true nature of the venture. He hopes that he can inspire you to not only invest in his scheme but to encourage others to do so as well, because *he* is the one who will make out big, and he knows it.

The simplest and least sophisticated of the pyramid schemes is the common chain letter. You have probably received a few yourself. If you understand how the chain letter works, you will better understand the more complicated scams.

THE CHAIN LETTER

Fred Detwiler was twenty-four years old, but lately he was feeling much older. He hated his office job. Looking at the postcards from his friends in Key West, Florida, which should have cheered him up, only made him feel worse. He wished *he* were there instead of being stuck behind a desk in Minneapolis, where the weather didn't agree with him. Neither did his boss when Fred suggested that he deserved a raise. Without a raise, he earned just enough money to make ends meet, not enough to save anything. At this rate he'd never get to Florida. Disgusted, he tossed the postcard and opened an anonymous-looking white envelope. As he began to read the enclosed letter, he perked up considerably:

Hello!

Don't junk mail me just yet—hear me out. This is my *third* time participating in this program. The first time (four months ago), I was very skeptical and only sent out 100 letters. I got 3,792 orders for a total income of $18,960! It shocked the livin' _____ out of me! That's not all. About six weeks ago, my wife and I sent out an additional 1,000 letters. Orders are still pouring in. . . .

To date we have received more than $87,000! That's right—$87,000!!! This third mailing will be 15,000 letters. In about three months from now, we will both quit our jobs, buy a home on the beach, and live off the interest on our money. . . .

Fred smiled. This was right up his alley. There was a lot more hype, but he was already sold. He leafed through the pages till he found the instructions for carrying out the "program":

FOLLOW THESE ACTIONS
TO ACHIEVE MAXIMUM RESULTS

1. Order all four reports from the advertisers on the list below by sending $5.00 IN CASH to each and a self-addressed, stamped envelope for fast reply. You will need all four reports as you will be reselling them. The act of reselling these reports satisfies legal requirements. Retype the names and addresses in the enclosed co-op list below, placing your name and address under ad number one. Move the name now under number one down to ad number two. Ad two name is moved to ad number three, and number three is moved to number four. The original name under ad number four is dropped off because he has already headed for the bank as you are preparing for your fortune.

2. After you have made all the above changes on the co-op list, take this letter to your local copier and have 200 or more copies made. (The average cost of 200 copies is $8.00.)

3. Send a copy of the enclosed material to small businesses, friends, classified advertisers, or best of all, get a hot name mailing list. Don't skimp in this department! A good list is well worth the investment. Postage for 200 letters at $.22 each comes to $44.00, and 200

number 10 envelopes can be purchased for less than $4.00.

Your total investment for all four reports plus the above comes to about $76.00. HERE'S HOW IT WORKS: You mail 200, and with only a 5 percent response, 10 will participate by mailing 200, increasing your ad to 2,000. Then 5 percent of those (or 100) participate by mailing 200 each, increasing your circulation to 200,000. Finally, with YOUR NAME on position four, 10,000 participate (5 percent of 200,000) by sending you $5.00 to order their reports. This totals a possible $55,000 for you with only a 5 percent response. Not bad for an investment of $76.00!

Not bad at all, Fred mused. He wondered who had sent him the letter, but didn't recognize any of the names in the four "positions" at the bottom of the page. Attached to the three-page chain letter was an advertisement for "High Quality mailing lists." These guys thought of everything! Funny, though, that the mailing list company was located in the same Texas town as the addresses in the four positions. And even though the letter stated that 200 names could be bought for nine dollars, the High Quality company offered a minimum of one thousand names for sixty dollars. Fred decided to get the names and addresses he needed from the telephone book.

Fred liked to think of himself as a pretty smart guy, but right now he was so eager to get his hands on some money that he never doubted the promises implicit in the chain letter. He wanted to believe them. It seemed plausible enough, all spelled out as it was. Besides, he liked the sound of the words *IN CASH*. If he were to get $55,000 in ones and fives, it would probably be too much to stuff into his suitcase. But who cared? He'd buy some kangaroo-skin luggage. And get the hell out of this cold, wet climate.

He called in sick the next morning and hurried down to the photocopy shop, letter in hand. He was told that the cost of two hundred copies was ten dollars, not eight dollars. Furthermore, since the letter he wanted to copy was three pages long, the cost to him would be thirty dollars. "Oh, yeah," Fred said, amazed that he hadn't thought of that before. But then, he was excited about this venture, which would mean the end of his nine-to-five grind and thus a ticket to freedom—at least for a while. He paid the thirty dollars and collected his sheaf of photocopies.

Next stop was the office supply store, where he learned that the least expensive business envelopes sold for $14.50 for a box of 250. That came to $10.50 more than the letter stated. Oh, well, Fred thought, shelling out the dough.

Back at home, he applied himself to sending for the "reports." He had to send five dollars to four different addresses; that was twenty dollars, as the letter indicated. What the letter didn't mention was that he would have to pay eighty-eight cents postage to send them and then another eighty-eight cents for four stamped, self-addressed envelopes. Lucky thing they came in boxes of 250; he wouldn't have thought of buying the eight additional envelopes.

Collating the pages of the letter, stuffing the envelopes, and finding and writing out two hundred names and addresses took much longer than Fred had expected. He called in sick the next day, too. It didn't really matter that these tasks were so time-consuming, though, because he had to wait until payday the following week before he could afford to buy the rest of the postage. Forty-four dollars' worth! Yeah, but it was worth it. He thought about how he would work on his tan.

Finally, everything was done. Fred dumped the two hundred letters into the mailbox in front of the post office with a feeling of satisfaction. It hadn't been easy, and it had ended up costing him $110.26, which was $34.26 more than the letter had indicated. Had he bought a mailing list he would have had to pay an additional sixty dollars. But now he was on easy street; all he had to do was sit back and wait for the cash to roll in.

The office routine seemed even duller than ever as Fred imagined what he'd be doing in a few weeks' time. He found himself daydreaming instead of working. Big deal, he reasoned. He wouldn't need this job much longer anyway. Soon he'd be dining on lobster in the Sun Belt. Maybe he would send a postcard to the old gang at the office. Then again, maybe not.

The days passed. Eventually, Fred received fifteen dollars through the mail, five dollars from three different people, but he had no reports to send back. Somehow, none of the people in the four positions had sent him any, although he was certain he had done everything according to the chain letter's specifications. Just as well; he didn't feel like sending out photocopies of the reports anyhow.

No more responses arrived, and gradually Fred forgot all about the chain letter. He was determined to apply himself to winning a lottery instead.

It isn't surprising that Fred didn't make out big with the chain letter. The area had already been milked by the time the mailman dropped a copy in Fred's mailbox. Look at it this way: Fred spent $110.26 just to send out his two hundred copies and buy his reports. In order to almost break even, he needed twenty-two people to send him five dollars. Had this happened, he would have been out only twenty-six cents. Assuming Fred's costs are about average, this means that for every participant to break even, twenty-two new people are necessary to continue the chain. Let's say that when Fred responded to the chain letter, he was one of a group of one thousand participants at the same stage of the chain (although thousands more had perhaps been contacted and had declined to get involved in the scheme). In order for those one thousand participants to almost break even, twenty-two thousand people would have had to continue the chain. For further "generations" of the letter, the figures would have to multiply as follows in order for all participants to almost break even:

484,000
10,648,000
234,256,000
5,153,632,000

For purposes of illustration, let's say that each of the one thousand people, who along with Fred continued the letter, sent out two hundred copies and that everyone who continued the letter thereafter—about 5 percent of those contacted—also sent out two hundred copies. Fred's group would contact two hundred thousand people. The number of people contacted would multiply as follows:

2,000,000
20,000,000
200,000,000
2,000,000,000

Looking at the figures above, it is easy to see that it would be impossible to keep the chain going through several generations in this way. The first figure, two million, equals the official 1981 population of Panama. The second figure, twenty million, is nearly three times the population of New York City. Compare the third figure, two hundred million, with the population of the United States (approximately 226,504,825) and you will get a feel for the scope of the undertaking. The fourth figure, two billion, is more than twice the population of China.

Now let's see how many new participants it would take for each of the one thousand people in Fred's group to realize the "possible $55,000" jackpot mentioned in the letter. For each person in the group, eleven thousand people would have to send in five dollars. This means that for Fred's group of one thousand people, eleven million new participants would be necessary to continue the chain. If every man, woman, and child in Ohio were to contribute five dollars each, Fred's group could just about make it, but not quite.

If anyone actually made the $55,000 goal, it was the first four people on the chain-letter list—the authors of the scheme. Assuming that these four collaborated, each sending out two hundred copies and then splitting their proceeds, and assuming for the sake of illustration that there was a 5 percent response rate, the figures would be as follows:

4		
40	x $5 =	$200
400	x $5 =	$2000
4,000	x $5 =	$20,000
40,000	x $5 =	$200,000

The enlisting of forty thousand or more people to continue a chain letter must be conceded to be an ambitious endeavor, regardless of the efficacy of the "High Quality" mailing lists.

During the past decade, dressed-up chain-letter scams have cropped up around the country with names like *Circle of Gold* and *Businessmen's Club*. Despite their fancy trappings, however, such schemes are no more likely to earn money for participants than are any other chain-letter enterprises, nor are any pyramid money-making schemes legal. Federal postage regulations prohibit all pyramid schemes that request the mailing of money or items of value, even if the item in question is only a pair of shoe laces, and most states have enacted laws forbidding pyramid money-making ventures.

DISTRIBUTORSHIPS: DARE TO BE GREAT

I don't drink, smoke, or play around. I'm just about perfect.

Glenn Wesley Turner

If there is any one person to thank for the proliferation of state laws concerning pyramid sales in the 1970s, it is Glenn Wesley Turner. Not that he set out to provoke a crackdown on pyramiding, of course. Quite the contrary. But he was so good at what he did; so stupendously successful, in fact, that he alerted lawmakers to the possibilities of pyramid distributorship rip-offs, thus indirectly ensuring that no future con artist would ever follow in his bootsteps.

Turner was fond of using his own life story to show what "the power of positive thinking" could do. He was, he said, proof that "all things are possible to him that believeth" (Mark 9:23).

The son of a poor, South Carolina sharecropper, born with a cleft lip which was never properly corrected, and schooled only through the eighth grade, Turner did start out at a disadvantage. The fact that he was able to overcome such impediments to financial success marks him as a sort of prodigy. He manipulated his audiences by professing to have great sympathy with the poor and downtrodden, and most of those who bought into his franchising system were in fact undereducated and in the lower financial brackets. Some of his concern for the unfortunate was probably sincere, however, as he was a heavy contributor to charities for the handicapped. Turner often said that he himself was handicapped; if he could whip his problems, others could whip theirs.

Turner went from job to job, more than twenty-six by 1967, without showing any particular flair or aptitude for any of them. For a time he sold sewing machines door-to-door to poor rural blacks. He then went broke working as a distributor for a small cosmetics firm. This gave him an idea, however. With a $5,000 bank loan, he began Koscot (Kosmetics for the Kommunities of Tomorrow) Interplanetary Inc., in Orlando, Florida. Even before he had the cosmetics on hand he had a small staff making the rounds to sell distributorships, or franchises, for $5,000 apiece. People began to buy, and Turner was on his way.

To see Turner disembark in grand style from a plane—he traveled the country at a rate of 500,000 miles a year—then climb into a waiting limo with the identically clad twin midgets who accompanied him everywhere, no one would guess that a few years earlier he had been a penniless and unobtrusive sewing-machine salesman. Officiating at Golden Opportunity meetings in local halls across the nation, he had the stage presence of a born actor and the persuasive powers of the born con artist. He was frequently compared in the press with the fundamentalist preacher Billy Sunday and the circus entrepreneur P. T. Barnum. As Turner appeared on stage, flanked by the loyal midget twins, the crowd would chant "Go-Go-Go-Go! Mmmmmmmmoney!" with hysterical enthusiasm. The sound has been likened to that of an oncoming locomotive. Meetings were frequently punctuated by members (possibly shills, or plants) standing up to "testify" or "witness" their own success in the program, thereby increasing the evangelical fervor of the performance.

Turner dressed with élan, sporting an oversized, rhinestone American-flag lapel pin and boots made from the hides of unborn calves. He had made hundreds of millions of dollars and wanted the world to sit up and take notice. More to the point, he wanted his audience, which was comprised mostly of individuals from underprivileged backgrounds, to see and identify with his success. Dare to rise above mediocrity, he exhorted them. Dare to be great!

Basically, this act of daring entailed shelling out $5,000 for what Turner called a distributorship. This amounted to a franchise in Glenn W. Turner Enterprises. To make a profit, the buyer was then entitled to recruit other distributors, keeping from $1,950 to $3,000 of each $5,000 fee for himself. The cost of becoming a supervisor was $2,000, of which the recruiter was entitled to keep $500. Distributors were given discounts on products. Forty percent of sales proceeds went to the salesperson and Glenn W. Turner Enterprises, and 10 percent each to the wholesale and retail franchiser.

Sales? What sales? Well, yes, products were sold, although in the rush to sell distributorships, they were often neglected. As Turner became increasingly successful, he began adding more companies. "Fashcot" dealt in wigs; "Emcot" dealt in pink and yellow fur coats; and "Transcot" was a trucking firm. The holding company, Glenn W. Turner Enterprises, eventually had more than seventy subsidiaries. "Dare to Be Great," the cassette-and-notebook training course, cost $5,000. Once the student had completed his course, he was allowed to recruit distributors and to collect $2,000 for each one he signed up.

By the early Seventies, the buying and selling of distributorships was still frenzied, but the writing was on the wall. People at the bottom of the pyramid were feeling the crush. They had financed those higher up and now were unable to find anyone left to recruit.

The franchising system of Glenn W. Turner Enterprises resembled a chain letter. Not only were sales distributorships far more lucrative than product sales, but franchise territories overlapped. No distributor had exclusive rights to an area. According to the New York State Attorney General's Office, in some cases there were as many as one thousand distributorships in a town of seven thousand people. The sales pitch delivered by Turner and his representatives did not jive with the realities of the situation. Koskot pitchmen stated, for example, that distributors and supervisors could earn $100,000 a year. The New York State Attorney General's Office declared, however, that of 1,604 distributors and supervisors in the state, only seventy-nine earned more than $5,000 a year from Koskot. For everyone then involved in the New York program to earn the promised one hundred grand, at least 150 million distributorships—eight apiece for every inhabitant of New York State—would have to be created.

Turner remained unperturbed in the face of growing skepticism and snowballing legal actions against him and his companies. Referring to his detractors as *Martians*, he kept up his song and dance, showing by his own example the power of positive thinking. Or, perhaps more accurately, the power of unmitigated chutzpah.

By 1973 the Federal Trade Commission (FTC), the Securities and Exchange Commission (SEC), and the U.S. Postal Department had all filed some sort of action against Turner and Glenn W. Turner Enterprises. At one time he faced fraud charges in all fifty states; 1,500 distributors filed lawsuits against him.

Turner, insisting that all of the lawsuits were part of a nationwide conspiracy to put him out of business, hired F. Lee Bailey as his lawyer and prepared to fight. Turner never did go to prison; he claimed that he beat almost 150 years of sentencing by means of appeals, spending more than $12 million in the process.

The SEC nevertheless brought down Turner's empire. Finding that an investment in a pyramid-distributorship scheme constitutes the offer and sale of a security, courts at federal and state levels found Turner guilty of neglecting to give investors full disclosure of the franchising system, as well as failure to register with the SEC.

And so Glenn Wesley Turner lost his empire; but all considered, he didn't come out too badly. By 1978 he had started Nature's World, a new cosmetics operation, avoiding pyramiding by giving away his franchises. One million dollars in debt to the IRS, he and his wife were still able to maintain the lifestyle to which they had become accustomed, living luxuriously with help from friends. Nor did Turner's self-confidence appear to be squelched by his downfall. He stuck to the story that he had been persecuted by a national conspiracy and continued to deny any responsibility for his alleged wrongdoings. Because he refused to contribute $200,000 to Richard Nixon's 1968 campaign, he said, the government made him a scapegoat by "coming after me with those indictments." Once again, the power of positive thinking came to his aid, according to Turner. He attributed his success in avoiding prison to the fact that he always believed that "poor, harelipped Glenn was right." By 1978 he had sufficiently recovered from his ordeal that he was ready, not only to become a multimillionaire again, but to dabble in politics as well. His ultimate goal? To become president of the United States.

Pyramid distributorship scams will doubtless continue to be perpetrated on the unwary, but never again on Turner's lavish scale. The public may forget Turner as the years pass; as P. T. Barnum remarked, "There's a sucker born every minute." But the court decisions and state laws inspired by the sharecropper's son from South Carolina will remain on the books to prevent would-be imitators from achieving his amazing success.

PONZI SCHEMES

Similar in principle to the chain letter, the Ponzi scheme has undergone many variations over the years, but when you dig down far enough past the promotion, the schemes are essentially the same.

Investing with Ponzi: The Original Scam

The name *Ponzi* has become synonymous with pyramid investment schemes just as *Kleenex* is synonymous with facial tissue. The story of Charles Ponzi's life is a rags-to-riches and back again saga unsurpassed in the annals of confidence artistry.

Born in the province of Emilia in northern Italy, he spent his first seventeen years on his parents' farm. The life of a farmer was not for him, however, and in 1899 he sailed from Naples to the United States to seek his fortune. His various attempts at making an honest living did not pay off, nor did his first attempts to make a dishonest living. In Montreal, at the age of twenty-five, using the surname *Bianchi*, he became involved in a con with an older man named Zarossi to bilk other Italian immigrants of funds that were supposed to be sent back to relatives in the old country. The clients received interest on their payments, but the relatives overseas never saw a lira of the principal. Young Bianchi did time (Zarossi had fled the scene by the time the law got involved), and then did some more time for a bungled attempt to smuggle two aliens across the Canadian border into the United States. Using the name Charles Ponzi, he started over again with a clean slate in Boston, Massachusetts.

Ponzi's first inkling of the scheme that was to make him a multimillionaire came in 1919, as he sat in the office of the J. P. Poole import-export brokerage house. A correspondent had sent him a postal reply coupon, purchased in Italy for the equivalent of one cent, which could be exchanged in the United States for five cents. These coupons were issued for the purposes of paying international return postage, but Ponzi thought that he could devise a more personally advantageous use for them. At thirty-seven, he was supporting a wife on the miserable wage of sixteen dollars a week, for which he had to kowtow to his superiors at Poole. If he could get an accomplice to buy postal coupons in Italy and then send them to him to sell at a 500-percent profit, he could be rich in short order.

Not long afterward, Ponzi was explaining his plan to his neighbors in the tenements and collecting fifty-dollar investments with the promise that within three months they would get seventy-five dollars back. Ponzi had a way with words, perhaps sharpened by his apprenticeship under Zarossi in Montreal, and he played on his so-called connections at the brokerage house. The coupon deal was a secret known only to himself and a few others, like, for instance, Rockefeller, he let on. It was a sure thing.

Emboldened by the future wealth he so clearly envisioned, Ponzi showed up an hour late for work one day, an unprecedented incident for him. Since he had begun his job at Poole, he had always been a paragon of punctuality and dependability. His tardiness, though, did not go unnoticed; his supervisor bawled him out, and, when Ponzi refused to show appropriate remorse for his misdeed, his supervisor threatened to fire him. Ponzi quit.

After his investors' three-month period was up, Ponzi's neighbors were reimbursed with interest not at 25 percent, as they had been guaranteed, but at 50 percent. They gladly reinvested the entire amount, and spread the word around the neighborhood that Charles Ponzi was the man with whom to do business. He was on his way to the big time.

Though Ponzi continued to use the postal-coupon exchange scheme, he had actually given up on even attempting to pursue that avenue. His research had shown him that only a limited number of coupons were issued each year, not enough to finance an investment system like the one he had in mind. So Ponzi borrowed from Peter to pay Paul, reimbursing earlier investors with funds taken from later investors. He had no trouble finding the increasing numbers of participants necessary to keep the operation going smoothly. His pitch, easy self-assurance (which in reality amounted to megalomania), and readiness to pay unheard-of interest rates, all contributed to his credibility. Happy investors convinced their friends that Ponzi's coupon business was a safe, easy, and quick way to multiply their savings.

Ponzi was in the investment business less than a year before the law caught up with him, but he and his wife Rose managed to accomplish a lot in the months between December 1919 and August 1920. Rose went to work as Ponzi's secretary. As the business skyrocketed, they rented a larger office and hired clerks to accept money and write out receipts. The flow of eager participants was constant. Busy clerks were instructed to record the amount of cash received from each participant and then chuck it into a wire basket. The sight of those baskets running over with money and the casual way in which the money was handled served to fan the investors' greed into a blaze. At the end of the day, Charles and Rose would pack the bills into suitcases and carry them to the bank.

Ponzi bought a mansion in Lexington, a suburb of Boston, and hired servants to run it. He could not, however, buy his way into society. On one occasion he and Rose invited the whole neighborhood to a huge feast, complete with bootleg liquor. After a couple of hours had passed, they got tired of waiting for their invited guests to arrive and Ponzi sent his car and a fleet of taxis to the old neighborhood to pick up their friends. They had no trouble persuading the tenement dwellers to come for a frolic in Lexington, where everyone partied until the wee hours of the morning, when the festivities were broken up by the police. If the suburbanites were too good to come to a party thrown by Italian immigrants, Ponzi reasoned, at least they were forced to take notice that they had missed a good bash.

Ponzi soon bought up most of the stock in the Hanover

Trust Company, gaining a controlling interest in the bank and becoming its president. He also bought out the J.P. Poole import-export brokerage and made a common daydream come true by firing the supervisor who had threatened to fire him. Ponzi made good on his promises to pay 50 percent interest on investments within forty-five days, and Boston reacted with a sort of frenzied greed. All told, he took in over $10 million in less than a year. The little Italian—Ponzi was only five foot two—was treated like a celebrity, and he loved his newfound popularity.

The original Ponzi scheme was not fated to last long, however. A concerted effort by the press forced the governor's office and the state attorney general to audit Ponzi's records. His personal charm and smooth talk, as well as his reputation, might have won the authorities over. No politician wanted to be known as the man who destroyed the chicken that laid the golden egg, especially with elections coming up. But the press ferreted out information on Ponzi's past crimes in Canada, and that was the beginning of the end.

Unable to sign on new investors while he was under investigation, Ponzi began "borrowing" from Hanover Trust Co., leaving IOUs for millions of dollars. He then tried to compound this money by gambling, a common tactic of con men, with the usual result: He lost it all.

There is no telling how long Ponzi's system could have kept going had there been no outside interference. Like all pyramid schemes, it was destined by its very nature to eventual failure. In any event, when Ponzi's empire crashed, several banks collapsed as well. Ponzi was jailed by the feds for violating the postal statutes (Rose had contacted investors by postcard to tell them their interest was ready to be collected, and this was interpreted as using the mails to defraud). After his release, he was sent back to do more time on a grand larceny conviction (the *People of Massachusetts* v. *Charles Ponzi*). In 1934, his time served, he was deported to Italy, without even the necessary funds to bring Rose with him.

They planned to reunite in Italy as soon as he could get the money together for the passage.

Rose continued to write faithfully for a while, but eventually Ponzi noticed a change in the frequency as well as the content of her correspondence. In an effort to earn her fare to Italy, he began to blackmail officials back in Boston with threats to publish damaging information about them in his autobiography. Ponzi had been unable to interest a publisher in such a book, but the politicians didn't know this, and Ponzi was able to rake in a small fortune. He also contacted the dictator Benito Mussolini, whom he admired, offering to handle press relations in Ethiopia. Mussolini granted Ponzi an audience, but was more intrigued with his American money-making scheme than in hiring him to go to Ethiopia.

Rose's Dear John letter was a long time in coming. She had waited for Charles for a long time. But by the time her husband was ready to send for her, she had finally had enough and was suing for divorce. He dropped his blackmail correspondence, went into a drunken decline, and probably would have died had he not received a belated offer from Mussolini to take over the business managership of the Latin Airlines in Rio de Janeiro. Ponzi accepted and prospered. At sixty, he was certainly not as wealthy as he had been at thirty-seven, but he earned enough to live in style and maintain two mistresses in Rio.

Ponzi's final downfall came when Mussolini was defeated. He lost his job, suffered a stroke, and, in 1949, died in a charity ward at the age of sixty-seven.

Big Names, Big Bucks, and Pink Pipes: The Home-Stake Oil Swindle

> *He [Trippet] is the biggest flimflam man ever to hit Wall Street.*
>
> William H. Morton
> former Home-Stake investor and
> president of American Express Co.

What do Jacob Javits, Ozzie Nelson, Bob Dylan, Walter Wriston (vice-president and chairman of CitiBank), Thurman Munson, Bobby Gentry, Alan Alda, David Cassidy, Ernest Hollings, Donald M. Kendall (chairman of PepsiCo Inc.), Barbra Streisand, and Nathaniel Goldstein (former attorney general of New York) have in common?

They were among the many big-name investors to be conned by Robert S. Trippet and his Tulsa-based Home-Stake Production Company.

Bob Trippet didn't fit most people's image of a con man. Straightforward, well mannered, low-key, from a prominent Texas family, he was as conservative and well-heeled as Glenn Wesley Turner was flamboyant and disadvantaged. Trippet knew how to use his credentials to divert suspicion from his business dealings; he was a pro at the soft sell, stall, and false show of righteous indignation when confronted with his scammy dealings. It was this skill that enabled him to continue his tax-shelter fraud for so long, for, unlike his predecessor, Charles Ponzi, Trippet never tried to make good on promises to investors. During the years 1955 to 1972, when Home-Stake Production was in operation, the company collected $140 million from investors and paid back $50 million. Long-term returns had been projected at 300 percent or above for each yearly tax-shelter program. The U.S. Treasury was also defrauded by Home-Stake, to the tune of $79,275,000.

A Ponzi or a Turner would never have been able to con such a sophisticated and knowledgeable clientele as Trippet's, mainly because neither had Trippet's background or connections. Wealthy from birth, Trippet came from an upright, well-respected family. His father had been a bank officer in Enid, Texas, a state banking officer in Bartlesville, Oklahoma, and president of Home Savings & Loan in Bartlesville. His maternal grandfather had been attorney general of Oklahoma in the days before it became a state. Trippet was a practicing lawyer wise in the ways of the IRS, the SEC, and the legal intricacies of the oil business. He had been an Eagle Scout in school, and his only brush with the law had been when, as a boy, he and some friends had rigged a vending machine at their country club.

Marrying into a wealthy family known as pioneers of the Oklahoma oil business, as well as for honesty and integrity, didn't hurt Trippet either. His brother-in-law, O. Strother Simpson, operated Home-Stake Oil & Gas Co., founded in 1917 by Simpson's grandfather, and Home-Stake Royalty Corporation, founded in 1929 by his father. When Bob Trippet started Home-Stake Production, he asked O. Strother Simpson to become its figurehead president, banking on gaining an automatic reputation by association. It paid off, too, although Simpson, unhappy with Trippet's questionable business ethics, resigned his post in 1958. The reason for Simpson's resignation was hardly common knowledge, however; after all, Bob Trippet was married to his sister, and Simpson didn't want to stir up unpleasantness in the family.

Trippet's system worked basically as follows. Every year Home-Stake sold a new oil-drilling program as a tax shelter for wealthy clients. Because the U.S. government wanted to encourage petroleum exploration, any money invested in an oil-drilling venture may be deducted from a citizen's taxable income. Therefore, an individual in the 50-percent tax bracket who invests $1,000 in a company like Home-Stake saves $500 in tax. Later, when he begins to make a profit from his investment, his oil income will be taxed at a lower rate than other income. Also, if the investor has retired by the time he starts to collect, his tax bracket will be lower and so he will save by having deferred paying his taxes.

Because money invested for purposes of drilling is deductible during the year in which the drilling takes place, Home-Stake offered yearly drilling programs. Trippet claimed that both his new wells and his secondary wells, in which oil was obtained by a process called waterflooding, were completely safe and reliable. The annual prospectus, a formal summary of the venture for investors which was required for disclosure by the SEC, was a useful tool to Trippet. Signed by a CPA and a lawyer, it looked convincingly official. The SEC did not check out the statements in the prospectus for accuracy, assuming that companies would basically tell the truth about their programs. This was not an assumption that could be safely made when dealing with Bob Trippet.

Trippet operated exactly as if everything he told his clients about Home-Stake were true, while using the money they invested for his own expenditures rather than to drill or waterflood oil wells. Some of the money was also used to pay investors minimal dividends. The rate paid per unit depended on the individual investor. When Trippet had a reason to want to remain in a participant's good graces, he would pay him at the highest rate. Others were paid much less, but no one received the projected amount. Trippet always had a ready excuse for participants who complained. Much of his job was public relations, and he was very good at this aspect of his work. He wrote personal letters to investors, answering questions, disseminating misinformation and outright lies, asking after their flower gardens and families. To those who wanted their money back, he suggested that they instead donate their units to charity. He had official reports assessing the value of the annual program units at much more than the prices investors had paid for them. These reports could be shown to the IRS so that participants could deduct more from their taxes than they had paid for the units, thus coming out ahead. Trippet had other dodges as well.

Very little of the money taken in by Home-Stake went to the purpose for which it was intended, but the company did have a few operating oil wells to show clients. They would be flown in by private plane, toured around the site, then whisked away to be lavishly entertained by Trippet and his vice-presidents, who were also his salesmen. This plan worked very well.

In some cases, clients were shown dummy wells. Trippet insisted that workers at one site make oil shoot out of a well against the rock face of a cliff. Home-Stake employees were to take photographs of this demonstration according to Trippet's explicit instructions: The photographer had to stand so that the shooting oil was featured in the foreground, in front of the excited celebrity investors. These photographs were used for publicity in Home-Stake's Black Book, an illegal document in which claims, so exaggerated that Trippet didn't dare exhibit them in the prospectus, were published for the benefit of present and future investors. At one site, a farming area, Trippet wanted to have fake oil derricks erected, but farmers objected on the grounds that they would interfere with crop dusting. Ingeniously enough, Home-Stake instead had overflow water irrigation pipes painted pink and labeled to imply that they were attached to production wells or to steam injection wells.

As the years passed, the number of dissatisfied customers increased, but somehow there were always more ready to invest. The names of investors, many of them big-time businessmen, had become Home-Stake's main selling point. Trippet soothed, cajoled, and occasionally intimidated worried participants. When these methods didn't work, he bought them out if he considered them powerful enough adversaries, or he offered them their initial outlay minus paid dividends and minus tax savings gleaned from deductions. No attempt was ever made to pay unhappy participants the interest on their money they might have made had their money been placed elsewhere. In some cases, Trippet simply refused to make any reimbursement.

Sometimes he threatened to sue investors who demanded their money back because they hadn't "fulfilled their contracted obligations to Home-Stake." In some cases this countermeasure worked, but not always. There were lawsuits against Home-Stake, which were handled out of court. Complaints made to the SEC by dissatisfied clients were largely ignored.

By 1973, Trippet saw that everything was about to hit the fan and decided to get out of Home-Stake while the getting was good. The company treasury contained $5.4 million, which would appeal to buyers. They wouldn't have to know, Trippet figured, the extent of their obligations to investors until after the sale.

It was interesting that, when Trippet did sell, it was to Elbert Myron Riebold, a renowned con artist in his own right. People who dealt with him said Riebold was charming, able to hypnotize his victims, and that no good had ever come of associating with him. Friends of Trippet warned him that Riebold had the reputation of a first-rate swindler, but Trippet did not appear to care one way or the other.

Riebold, for his part, seemed most concerned about the cash he would be able to funnel out of Home-Stake into other endeavors. He had just transferred the funds to Denver, where he planned to move Home-Stake (this would also have been in Trippet's best interests, as it would have covered up his tracks to some extent) when the SEC pounced. Home-Stake was declared insolvent, and legal proceedings were begun.

The trials associated with the Home-Stake oil swindle were not concluded until 1977. Millions of dollars were still unaccounted for, and most investors never recouped any portion of their lost principal. To add insult to injury, the IRS retroactively changed the deduction status of the charitable donations, which meant that for many participants tax-shelter gains were lost as well.

What happened to Bob Trippet, now that he was finally caught in his own sticky web of deceit and subterfuge? Not much. He pleaded *nolo contendere* (no contest) and was convicted of one count of conspiracy to defraud and nine counts of mail fraud. For these offenses, he was sentenced to one day in jail, three years of supervised probation, a fine of $15,000, and a fine of $100,000 to be paid into a fund for investors made destitute by Home-Stake, with the provision that any money unclaimed by qualified applicants after a certain time would be returned to Trippet. The presiding judge appeared to consider the fund something of a joke; he showed little sympathy for Trippet's rich and famous clients. A wealthy man before and after his conviction, Bob Trippet did not fare too badly. Which just goes to show that if you're going to rip people off, it's a good idea to be a white-collar crook.

"Mr. Excitement on Wall Street"

Dennis Greenman, known in his heyday as "Jaws" and "Mr. Excitement on Wall Street," is now referred to by SEC officials as "the Ponzi of the computer age."

Greenman had a great deal in common with Bob Trippet. Both had respectability and financial backing to ease their way in the business world. Both were quiet, outwardly conservative, and soft-spoken. Greenman is said to have the kind of eyes that inspire trust in anyone who will meet his gaze. Both had the education, intelligence, skills, and connections to earn a fortune by honest means, had they been willing to settle for it. But there are men who can't seem to abide by the rules. Trippet and Greenman couldn't stay out of the fast lane, even though eventually they were certain to get caught. Both used props to snow and mislead investors. Trippet had his Black Book and phony prospectus, Greenman a phony computer printout. Both invented and perpetrated elaborate Ponzi schemes. Greenman, however, as we shall see, paid a heavier price for his finagling than did Trippet.

When he entered the brokerage business in Florida in 1977, Greenman was already known as a computer genius.

A quiet, introspective sort, he at first seemed better able to communicate with electronic brains than with people. This computer compatibility was more a help than a hindrance to his career. Greenman worked for and with such prestigious firms as Merrill Lynch, Paine Webber, and A. G. Becker.

Using Barclay Financial Corporation, a discount brokerage firm in Miami, as a clearinghouse, he made a great deal of money in a short time, presumably at arbitrage. (Arbitrage is the buying and selling of stock-option contracts. A stock-option contract is the agreement to buy or sell a certain stock at a future time at a specific price.) Aided by his trusty computers, Greenman could complete a purchase or sale at any exchange in the United States in about two minutes. Because prices varied slightly among the exchanges, he could make profits several times a day on stock options by simultaneously buying and selling; he would buy an option on one exchange and immediately sell it at a higher price on another exchange.

For example, say a certain stock is selling for $100 on the Pacific Stock Exchange and, at the same time, for $102 on the New York Stock Exchange. The computer executes a simultaneous buy order on the Pacific exchange and a sell order on the New York exchange, thus picking up two points.

Greenman would cash out at the end of the trading day, converting all the money into Treasury bills for the night. Dealing as he did with millions of dollars, the small price differences among the exchanges added up significantly.

At least, this was Greenman's story. While he did start out wih arbitrage, Greenman began to get bored with its limited possibilities and looked around for more interesting games to play. Soon he was gambling with investors' money in risky call options (in which one essentially wagers that the price of an option one has bought will rise by a specific date). Hugo L. Black, Jr., a court-appointed receiver for Barclay, says that Greenman was paying himself "obscene commissions," placing so many orders in the Chicago options market that brokers called him "Jaws." As new investors poured in their money, Greenman used it to pay off old investors.

In order to accommodate his preferred clients in his "short-term trading program," Greenman started partnerships, exclusive clubs for investors. Membership was by invitation only; members had to invest at least $100,000 each for the privilege.

Greenman found other ways to use the computer as a tool of deception. He was keeping two sets of books, one accurate, the other fake. False monthly financial statements, bearing the logos of the Paine Webber and A. G. Becker companies, and showing 80 to 90 percent gains on investments, were mailed out to delighted investors. The statements were fakes, put out by Greenman's minicomputer. Greenman knew that even experienced, sophisticated businessmen who were much too sharp to believe everything they read *would* believe anything he sent them on a computer printout. They wouldn't even expect to understand it, but they would trust it. Everybody knows that computers don't make mistakes, especially in the hands of a renowned electronics and financial whiz like Greenman. To many people, computers represent technology at its most advanced level, and thus the phony printout is a better confidence tool than an embossed document with a raised seal, ribbons, and official signatures.

Greenman's scam was uncovered by the combined efforts of the FBI, SEC, and U.S. Department of Justice Strike Force in early 1981. While they knew enough to suspect wrongdoing, it took authorities about a month to figure out just *what* Greenman was doing wrong and how he was doing it. There were no witnesses to clue them in, no conspirators or partners to give away the game. Greenman was a one-man show, and he kept things to himself.

Charged with fraud, Greenman pleaded guilty and was sentenced to ten years in prison—a much harsher penalty than the slap on the wrist Trippet received for his investment schemes. Of the $80 million Greenman had taken in, only $27 million was retrieved.

"The real culprit is greed," an official of a New York brokerage firm commented. "Everybody wants to get in on the beginning of a pyramid scheme—but nobody wants to get in on the end."

That is, if they're smart.

9.

Snake Oil: Medical Quackery

The American people, according to P. T. Barnum, love to be humbugged. In pharmacy, his charge seems certainly true. The glamor of false pretenses in flaming advertisements attracts the ignorant and gullible as a bright light does a moth. . . . When this is associated with lying guarantees of quality without a vestige of doubt in the probity of the charlatan, they rush to him with their cash, as if he were a public benefactor. They never dream of the fact that he is quietly fleecing them before their very eyes.

R. G. Eccles, M.D.
The Druggists Circular and Chemical Gazette

A term for quackery, or health-care fraud, *snake oil* may not be an honorable profession, but it is certainly an ancient and very lucrative one. In hope of achieving a cure for every ailment from arthritis to zinc deficiency, the American public is still being humbugged much as it was one hundred years ago.

WHY PEOPLE FALL FOR QUACKS

If you think about it, it's easy to see why the snake-oil

purveyor has achieved such tremendous monetary success over the ages. We mortals are faced with the grim reality that we will either grow old or die, or else grow old and *then* die. But aging and death are not comfortable prospects to contemplate. A snake-oil con artist claims that he can restore youthfulness and cure terminal illness. He also promises miraculous remedies for chronic pain. Many times he sounds more convincing and encouraging than does his legitimate counterpart in the medical profession. This is because the quack is not hampered by professional ethics; he is not honor-bound to tell the truth. He is thus free to tell his patients what they want to hear.

Those who suffer from chronic, painful conditions are those who are most often victimized by quacks, who unashamedly hawk vitamins, medicines, diets, and exercise regimens guaranteed to cure arthritis, cancer, diabetes, and heart disease. The quack also panders to those who seek eternal youth, offering potions, lotions, pills, and gadgets purported to restore lagging energies and rejuvenate the body. Wrinkles, baldness, graying hair, age spots, cellulite . . . you name it, the snake-oil doctor has a surefire cure.

Some snake-oil victims are perfectly healthy, but susceptible to suggestion. Easily suggestible, they are also roped in by intimidation. The quack lists a number of vague "symptoms," which he maintains are signs of impending disease. Sometimes he even goes so far as to invent the disease, then convince the mark that he is suffering from it. If he is a con artist worthy of the name, he can then persuade the mark that he has cured him of the imaginary disease!

The hypochondriac, who for some reason *prefers* to be sick, is another rich source of revenue for the medical flimflam man. The hypochondriac eventually tires of bona fide medical practitioners; there is only so much an honest physician or psychologist can do for him. After he has received all the serious attention he can get from the legitimate medical community, the hypochondriac discovers the quack with delight. Here is someone willing to listen, diagnose, and prescribe for as long as it takes! The quack and the hypochondriac form a symbiotic bond: The quack's role is to pay attention; the hypochondriac's role is to pay cash. Usually he considers it well spent, for he enjoys going to the doctor more than going to the movies.

A quack may sometimes, quite coincidentally, help someone who is truly ill. Mind and body work together, and there is evidence that a person's belief that he will be cured is sometimes enough to cause him to "heal himself." This phenomenon is called the *placebo effect.* Voodoo has been known to cure and kill believers; some hypnotists have demonstrated the ability to eradicate warts by suggestion; and a doctor's bedside manner may hasten or hinder a patient's recovery. The placebo effect may also be set into motion by an extremely convincing snake-oil "doctor."

There is one further, and very obvious, reason why a quack may appear to cure his patients. Most diseases run their course, and the tendency of the body is toward healing. A quack often takes credit for the patient's own natural healing process—that is, if he doesn't actually damage the patient's health with his "remedies." The patient, convinced he has been helped, then ropes in his friends for the quack to treat.

DANGERS OF QUACKERY

At this point it may appear that the quack does more good than harm by offering hope in otherwise hopeless cases, lending an ear to the hypochondriac who wants attention, and perhaps, by means of the placebo effect, providing the suggestion that helps the patient to heal himself. The dangers of snake oil are, however, very real.

By siphoning off the savings of those who cannot afford

expensive and ineffective cures, the quack impoverishes his patients, making their lives more uncomfortable than before. He also may deplete a patient's savings to the extent that good medical care is no longer affordable.

Another danger of quackery is that it often postpones or takes the place of bona fide medical care. Having discovered that he has been swindled, the patient goes to a physician, only to discover that he has contracted permanent damage— damage which would have been preventable had he sought legitimate health care in the first place.

Finally, the medicines, megavitamins, and diets dictated by quacks are frequently harmful in themselves. So-called health regimens are often completely unsuitable for the diseases and conditions for which the medical con artist prescribes them; ingredients in herbal teas and other remedies are sometimes poisonous. It is a common error, both on the part of the customer and the snake-oil salesman himself, to believe that natural plant products and medicinal herbs are necessarily mild and benign. Foxglove and lily of the valley, used for centuries in folk medicine, contain digitalis, a drug that affects heart rate. Celandine, a little yellow wildflower, is cousin to the opium poppy and possesses similar narcotic properties. Those who doggedly maintain that herbs can't hurt should remember that nicotine, cyanide, and belladonna are all natural, organic drugs derived from plants and used for centuries in folk remedies. In the hands of people who don't understand their uses, these organic substances can be deadly.

In 1982 a California-based, herbal diet-aid company was sent a notice of adverse findings by the Food and Drug Administration (FDA). One of the company's products contained pokeroot and mandrake, plants considered unsafe for human consumption. FDA officials pointed out that mandrake was once used by American Indians as a suicide drug.

WHEN TO SUSPECT SNAKE OIL

None of us wants to be taken in by the snake-oil doctor, but for the inexperienced it is difficult to recognize him. He hides behind a facade of respectability or plays the part of a medical crusader. Whatever his gimmick may be, he will try his best to persuade the public that he is an honest and competent healer. How can we spot him for what he is?

The FDA has issued the following warning signs of quackery. Beware the snake-oil salesman when:

- a service or product is touted as a secret remedy.
- a medicine, dietary supplement, or product is flogged by a traveling salesman or sales team, either door-to-door or through promotional lectures.
- a product is promoted in a sensational manner in a magazine advertisement, by a faith-healing group, or by a crusading organization of laymen.
- the product or service is advertised as a panacea, or multipurpose cure, "good for what ails you."

You should also be leery when medical promoters:

- base their claims on vague, pseudoscientific theories; poorly documented research studies and case histories; studies conducted by organizations with grand-sounding, but untraceable, names; or emotional testimonials by people claiming to have used the product or service.
- base their claims on exotic, unorthodox, or faddish techniques and philosophies that you cannot research.
- attempt to convince you to buy a product or treatment that you would not have considered had you not heard the sales pitch, or to persuade you that, although you feel healthy, you have several ambiguous symptoms of a disease only they can successfully treat.
- sell a cure for arthritis, cancer, diabetes, or heart disease.

- complain of persecution by the AMA or government authorities.

FAKE CREDENTIALS

It is a good idea to check out the credentials of a doctor before entrusting him with your mind, body, or hard-earned cash. If the diplomas on your doctor's wall are from Mediterranean, Central American, or South American countries, be wary. While such diplomas may be valid, there is also a possibility that they may have come from a diploma mill. (Medical schools in some of these countries will sell diplomas; for the right price, a layman can buy full credentials as a man of medicine.)

If you have been fooled by sham credentials and puffed-up résumés, you are certainly not the first. Almost anyone can be bluffed, including heads of state and hospital personnel.

The former Queen Juliana of the Netherlands was twice misled by confidence men posing as psychiatrists. During the Sixties, Greet Hoffman became the Queen's confidant. The mind games he played with the monarch put her under his sway and kept her there, much to the outrage of the Dutch public, until he was exposed as a sham and ousted from his privileged post. Then, in the Seventies, the royal dressmaker introduced Queen Juliana to another bogus shrink, the Baron David James Rothschild. Nobody, aside from the dressmaker, knew that he was a poseur whose real name was Henry de Vries. (The former laborer was sharing an apartment with the dressmaker when the scam was hatched.) He must have had quite a way about him, as Queen Juliana appointed him as her psychiatrist and spent many an hour talking with him at the Soestdijk Palace in the Hague. De Vries became so comfortable in his new position that he slipped up. In 1978 he applied for a permit to hold a party on the palace grounds. His papers were duly checked by the bureaucracy; in the paper-shuffling process, his true identity was discovered. De Vries speedily dispatched himself to France, and once again the monarch was left with no one to listen to her troubles. Which just goes to show it's lonely at the top, even in the Netherlands.

In the United States, there have been many cases of impersonators with no previous medical experience or training who fob themselves off as physicians. The surprising thing about these cons is how readily they are accepted by trained medical personnel. Barry Vinocur, a college dropout with the gift of gab, snowed the employment department at a hospital in Ohio and got a job as a medical technician. He did well in this position, despite his lack of schooling. Later he used his cousin's medical records to forge a physician's license. Vinocur read voraciously and watched the physicians at the medical faculty of the University of California in order to educate himself. He saved a baby's life at that institution by correctly diagnosing a rare blood disease. He was entrusted with the supervision of a land-and-helicopter lifesaving operation for newborns. With three doctors, he coauthored a textbook on intensive-care medicine.

In 1980 Vinocur's deceit was uncovered. Because he had done more good than harm in his chosen field, he was sentenced to a probation term and ordered to perform one hundred hours of community work without pay.

HISTORY OF SNAKE OIL

Voltaire once wrote that quackery has existed since the first knave met the first fool. Times change, and with them the quack's approach to selling his wares and services. But the game has remained basically the same over hundreds of years.

Alchemists

During the sixteenth through the eighteenth centuries, the

art of alchemy was given credence, even by many educated people. The notion that an alchemist could turn base metals into gold and concoct elixirs capable of eternally preserving youth and beauty was very popular then. Never missing an opportunity, the con artist took advantage of the widespread belief in alchemy to line his pockets.

One of the great alchemist con artists was Count Allessandro di Cagliostro, who amazed the royal courts of Europe with his magic health and beauty potions. Born Giuseppe Balsamo in Sicily in 1743, the son of penniless parents, he devoted his youth to removing himself from the slums. He seized the opportunity to rob his uncle and the church poor box and thus pay his fare out of Sicily. After wandering around for a time, he settled in Rome, where he made a living as a versatile grifter. He made and sold beauty ointments and love potions, and also engaged in counterfeiting, copying paintings, and other kinds of forgery. There he married a beautiful fifteen-year-old girl named Lorenza Feliciani. If her background was as undistinguished as his own, she was also nearly as talented as her husband, exhibiting a flair for acting that might have made her a stage queen under different circumstances.

The Balsamos soon wore out their welcome in Rome and moved on to practice their con games in southern Europe and northern Africa. In 1777, when Lorenza was in her late twenties and Giuseppe thirty-four, they made their appearance in London. All of their ill-gotten gains had been invested in fine clothes, jewelry, luxurious state-of-the-art coaches, and servants. The pair had learned that style is everything when you're out to make the big time. Giuseppe Balsamo was now Count Cagliostro, world traveler and alchemist, while Lorenza was transformed into Countess Serafina. Dazzled by her dark beauty, the Count said he had stolen her from an Oriental harem and taken her for his bride. The fabulous wealth they displayed was the result of the Count's ability to turn inexpensive metals into pure gold—or so ran their story.

In London, Cagliostro joined the Freemasons, an organization the membership of which included the wealthiest and most powerful men in Europe. This "club" was useful to the Count when he wanted to make contacts in England and abroad. In Paris, he initiated a new order of Freemasonry, the Egyptian rite. As head of the order, he was able to collect large sums of money in membership dues and initiation fees. For Countess Serafina, he started a women's branch so that she could con the ladies while he was conning their husbands. She divulged the secret of her youth and beauty to a few new friends: Although she was sixty years old, she said, the Count had formulated a cream that made her look thirty. When the ladies begged her for the chance to buy this wonderful cream, she was able to convince her husband to make up a few batches—strictly as a favor, of course. And the ladies swore by it, believing that they were cheating Father Time with the miraculous discovery. They promised to keep the Countess's beauty aid a secret, and yet somehow word got around.

Beauty cream was not the only source of revenue for the couple. The Count made herbal pills and wrapped them in gold leaf for his wealthy, titled clients, promising wonderful cures. Perhaps it was due to the packaging, but the pills became a great vogue around the courts of Europe, and the Count became the most sought-after doctor on the continent.

The Count was also a great success in Russia. According to one account, one of the Czar's ministers begged Cagliostro to cure his brother of insanity. The man was brought before him, securely bound, as extreme violence was one of the symptoms of his disease. Cagliostro ordered the bonds removed; when the man was free, he rushed at Cagliostro to attack him. Undaunted, the Count had him thrown into an icy river. After the minister's brother was eventually fished out, he purportedly acted and spoke in a sane and rational manner, apologizing to the Count and thanking him for restoring his senses.

By 1780 Count Cagliostro was so full of himself that he gave free rein to his imagination. He claimed that he was born before the Deluge, that he had discussed matters of state with King Solomon, Moses, and Socrates, and had partaken of a wedding feast in Cana, Galilee. No matter how preposterous his stories became, most people went right on swallowing them. After all, wasn't he effecting miracle cures in cases where other eminent doctors had failed? The French government, having a problem with some of the Count's tales, set up a board of doctors and scientists to investigate his cures. They ended up shrugging their shoulders. While they were unable to discover any scientific explanation for the Count's success with his elixirs, pills, and potions, the results seemed to be real. Former patients gave him glowing testimonials.

By 1785, Cagliostro's fame had reached superstar heights. Then a bum rap undermined his career: Accused of involvement in a conspiracy (the Diamond Necklace Affair) to forge the name of Marie Antoinette on documents, he and Serafina were thrown into prison. Later, when the pair was found innocent, crowds thronged the streets to celebrate their release. But the harm had already been done. Under questioning, Serafina had told her husband's secrets, and King Louis XVI was informed of her testimony. The "Count" and "Countess" were banished from France.

Back in Rome, the poor Balsamos again, the couple scrambled for ways to reinstate the lifestyle to which they had become accustomed. Giuseppe attempted to found another Egyptian rite Freemason order. But Freemasonry was strictly forbidden by the Pope, and in 1789 Balsamo was arrested, tried, and sentenced to death. Lorenza, who had denounced her husband in order to save her own skin, was shunted off to a nunnery for the rest of her life. The Pope commuted Balsamo's sentence to life imprisonment, and in 1795, at the age of fifty-two, he died in an Italian dungeon.

Golden Age of Quackery

In the United States, the nineteenth century was a marvelous period for quacks and self-prescribers of every stripe. Opiates and cocaine were freely available over the counter until the Harrison Narcotic Act was passed in 1914. Housewives included laudanum and paregoric in their home remedies, and chewing gums, wine, and soft drinks contained enough cocaine to give the user a buzz. (In the South, bottles of Coca Cola were known as "dopes" because of their drug content.) Before Theodore Roosevelt's Pure Food and Drug Act was passed in 1906, patent-medicine manufacturers were neither required to list ingredients on their labels nor to divulge their ingredients for any reason. The customer knew only what the salesman told him about the medicinal properties of the tonics, remedies, and liniments.

Snake-oil hucksters peddled their wares from town to town, making their biggest sales at carnivals and fairs. Popular patent medicines were sold in pharmacies nationwide, advertised in newspapers and magazines as panaceas for the whole spectrum of bodily ailments.

The style and mood of these newspaper advertisements is illustrated by this excerpt from an ad for Lydia E. Pinkham's Vegetable Compound: "A fearful tragedy, clergyman killed by his own wife. . . . Insanity brought on by 16 years of suffering with female problems the cause. Lydia E. Pinkham's Vegetable Compound, the sure cure for these complaints, would have prevented the direful deed."

The use of the term *snake oil* as a general term for quack medicines derives from the fanciful names given to patent medicines during this period. Two of the most famous of these old-time concoctions are Swamp Root and Kickapoo Oil.

Swamp Root was the brainchild of brothers Andral and Jonas M. Kilmer, who began their pharmaceutical career in New York in 1879. By 1912, the Kilmer family fortune was estimated at somewhere between $10 and $15 million, all gleaned from sales of patent medicine.

The brothers were full of imaginative names for their products, which included Indian Cough Cure, Autumn Leaf Extract for Females, Ocean Weed Heart Remedy, and Prompt Parilla Liver Pills. The most successful of all, however, was Swamp Root, advertised as "the great kidney, liver, and bladder remedy." In the 1905 *Swamp Root Almanac* published by Andral and Jonas Kilmer, this "remedy" was recommended even to those who felt perfectly fit. According to the almanac, such people were probably living in a fool's paradise. Prefaced by the slogan "Thousands have kidney trouble and don't know it!" was a list of fifty-six symptoms, most of them so vague and so common that almost any reader might infer that he was sicker than he had thought.

After the Food and Drug Act was passed, the Kilmers' company was under pressure to amend its labeling, which many believed to be misleading. In 1910 the claims on the label were no longer so exaggerated, but they were still inaccurate. According to a newspaper editorial of the times, the new label was "a model of deceptiveness and fraudulent intent, but which, nevertheless, does not lie specifically enough to bring it within the scope of the law." Advertising continued to be outrageous. Readers were advised to take a urine sample and allow it to stand overnight. If, by morning, sediment had settled to the bottom of the container, kidney disease was said to be indicated.

The U.S. Postal Service launched an investigation in 1912, and found that settling sediment indicated neither kidney disease nor anything else out of the ordinary. In fact, anyone who tested his urine in this manner would discover that he was in need of Swamp Root, at least according to the Kilmer literature. Due to pressure from the Postal Service, claims for Swamp Root became more subdued.

Despite the deaths of its creators, Swamp Root was so popular that it outlived them for several years. (Family members ran the factory during this time.)

The creators of Kickapoo Oil were two wild West showmen named Doc Healy, alias Colonel Healy, and Charles H. Bigelow, alias Texas Charlie. Their gimmick was to hype their medicines as "natural" Indian cures, made of roots, barks, gums, leaves, and berries. In reality, the Kickapoo Indian Medicine Company was an urban business, with offices in New York and St. Louis, and the ingredients were no more natural than those in any other patent medicines. Doc Healy and Texas Charlie advertised their products by going out on the road with them; and when they traveled, they traveled in style. During the years 1875 through 1880, they rode in a brightly colored, horse-drawn wagon, surrounded by an entourage of hired performers, most of whom were Indians. A sidekick known as Nevada Ned played the part of Chief Thundercloud. Indian dances were performed, and the medicines were hawked to crowds of onlookers. Although the Kickapoo Indian Medicine Company boasted a large line of patent medicines, Kickapoo Oil, a liniment, was far and away the most popular. Before 1906, it was advertised as a "quick cure for all kinds of pain, good for man or beast." After the Pure Food and Drug Act made such claims illegal, Kickapoo Oil was more modestly labeled "for aches and pains." When, according to law, the ingredients were listed on the label, they proved to be less natural than Doc Healy and Texas Charlie had led the public to believe. Whatever may have been the merits of Kickapoo Oil, the public loved it, and Doc Healy and Texas Charlie grew rich from proceeds of the Kickapoo Indian Medicine Company.

HISTORY REPEATS ITSELF

Successful con games go in and out of style. Once a con is outmoded, it goes into the closet for a few years, to be brought out again and dusted off for reuse. This is as true of health fraud scams as any other kind of con.

Electrical Gadgets

Back in the early 1900s, Dr. Albert Abrams astonished the American public with the news that he had discovered a way to diagnose and cure hitherto incurable diseases using electricity. Dr. Abrams was exposed as a quack, but that didn't stop others from following in his footsteps. In 1954 it came to the attention of the U.S. Postal Service that an elderly Idaho osteopath named Horace Biggley was selling a miraculous electrical device by mail order. Called the Magnetron, the device could be plugged into an ordinary outlet in any home. The patient had only to turn it on, take hold of a handle, and place his foot on an attachment pad. The panel on the Magnetron lit up, and a tiny amount of electricity—less than one would receive from an electric blanket—would be administered. The Magnetron, said Dr. Biggley, would cure prostate dysfunctions, varicose veins, arthritis, ulcers, diabetes, heart failure, and hemorrhoids. In trying to put together a case against Biggley, postal inspectors discovered that he was a follower of Abrams. Although Abrams had been discredited long before, Biggley remained faithful to Abrams' precepts—or thought that he could use them to make his fortune.

Biggley was brought to trial and acquitted, because, useless as the Magnetron proved to be, the prosecution was unable to show that he had intended to defraud. Postal inspectors had located and interviewed fifty Magnetron buyers, in hopes of getting them to testify against the osteopath. No dice. Most of the patients, many of whom were in poor physical condition, loved their Magnetrons. They preferred the device to conventional treatment, considering it less expensive and handier than going to the doctor.

A Boulder, Colorado, physician stated recently that Boulder is the modern center of health quackery; there is no place in the United States, except for parts of California, he believes, that even comes close to equaling the variety and number of cases of amateur medical malpractice in this city. It is no wonder, then, that gadgets similar to Abrams' and Biggley's have recently shown up at the foot of the Rockies.

In 1981, a Boulder publisher, experiencing muscle pain in his neck, visited a chiropractor in hopes of receiving a massage. The chiropractor positioned the publisher on a couch, and set up a small box next to his head and shoulders. He then left the room for several minutes, telling his patient that the device would alleviate the muscle pain. Alone with the mysterious box, which contained a blinking red light and emitted a low, whirring sound, the publisher grew both curious and suspicious. Upon turning it over, he found that it contained only the light mechanism and a small battery-operated machine that did nothing more than produce the whirring noise.

The publisher confronted the chiropractor with his discovery and told him that he would not pay for such an obvious rip-off. When the chiropractor insisted on payment, the publisher agreed, but, still holding the device, said that in that case he would just bring it along to show the district attorney. The chiropractor decided to take back his box and defer payment.

Persistent Purgatives

Oddly enough, every so often the use of the enema as a cure-all comes into vogue. Its medical benefits fall into disrepute, then crop up again. The self-styled chiropractor, Roy DeWelles, improved on the basic enema technique, adding an oxygen tank to a "colonic irrigation" machine and labeling the resultant contraption the Detoxicolon. The Detoxicolon had a lot more class than the usual enema paraphernalia, or so many patients seemed to think. In the twenty-year period from the early Forties through the early Sixties, during which time he was promoting the Detoxicolon procedure, DeWelles was a great success, convincing thousands of people that all diseases begin in the colon and can be cured by Detoxicolon therapy.

He operated through chiropractic offices, selling his machines for about $2,400 each to chiropractors and naturopaths. (Naturopathy is a system of disease treatment that relies solely on "natural" remedies, such as sunlight, diet—and colonic irrigation.) He would saturate the mails with advertisements to the residents of whatever town he happened to be visiting, offering free examinations by a "famous diagnostic specialist." Performing these exams himself, DeWelles would then tell the patient, no matter what his condition, that he needed a $10 X ray of his colon and lower stomach. In almost every case, these X rays were said to show that the patient was hatching some dread disease or was already afflicted. The solution to his condition: Detoxicolon treatment. Three months of weekly irrigation, at $350, was recommended for a "guaranteed cure." (Those who paid in advance got a $50 reduction.) DeWelles signed up patients, collected his fees, and left the chiropractor to administer the treatments.

When seizure actions were instituted against DeWelles in five federal districts in 1959 and 1950, he skipped to the Sunshine State. He instituted seventeen clinics in Florida in 1955, then skipped again with $100,000, one step ahead of the authorities.

In 1957 he classed up his operation further by hiring two semiretired physicians to lend credence to his detoxification operation in Los Angeles. There he was indicted on charges of criminal conspiracy to cheat and defraud after it became known that he was routinely treating cancer patients on the Detoxicolon. He and his associates were acquitted.

It was in Indiana in 1962 that DeWelles finally met his Waterloo. The local sheriff arrested DeWelles for practicing chiropractic without a license; X rays were seized from the clinic as a result of the arrest. Fraud was finally proved when it was demonstrated that the X rays of individual patients did not reveal the diseases that DeWelles had diagnosed and pretended to treat. He was sentenced to ten years in a federal penitentiary.

Then, in January 1978, in respected newspapers across the nation, the Midwest Health Research Laboratory began advertising a handbook entitled *Modern Solutions to Age Old Physical Problems*. Techniques for the prevention and cure of forty diseases, among them arthritis, diabetes, and hardening of the arteries, were said to be explained in the handbook, which cost $9.95. At least one thousand people bought a copy.

The handbook turned out to be a pamphlet. Inside was the amazing, secret cure for all disease—colonic irrigation! Customers could order their very own colonic irrigation kits from Midwest Health for only $29.95.

Shane G. Brannson III, AKA Robert B. Goode, was indicted on eighteen federal criminal counts as the instigator of the Midwest Health scam. He was convicted of two counts, to which he pleaded guilty as a result of plea bargaining, and was sentenced to three years in prison and a subsequent four-year probation period.

Here we are in the Eighties, and once again, the enema approach to health is back, this time pitched as a natural means of eradicating gallbladder stones. Using a technique similar to that of the old-time Swamp Root promoters, a

Boulder chiropractor is currently disseminating a pamphlet which warns that you may have gallstones and obstructions and not know it.

"Many people, even in their teens living in our society today fail to have free, unabstructed (sic) flow of bile from the gall bladder in response to food entering the small intestine," the pamphlet reads. "Eating refined or processed foods, fresh food which is mineral deficient because it was grown in depleted chemically treated soil, lack of vigorous exercise, stress, multiple distractions during meals, and many other unnatural aspects of our lifestyle have combined to alter the chemistry of bile so that formation of solid particles from bile components is a commonplace occurance (sic) among Americans."

The chiropractor author goes on to explain how those who suspect they may have formed solid particles from bile components can cause them to be speedily ejected from the gallbladder.

A long, drawn-out procedure is outlined, involving the use of many beverages, such as freshly extracted vegetable juices, apple juice, fenugreek and star anise tea, as well as foods like sprouts and yogurt. The most important part of the regimen, however, consists of three separate "flushes," two of which involve coffee enemas. (The coffee enema is in itself a health hazard.) But first, olive oil (the chiropractor recommends cold-pressed, unrefined olive oil) and lemon juice must be drunk in alternating doses, one-half cup of each. Nausea, he cautions, is often experienced, and may last for several days, but this discomfort is a sign that your gallbladder needed to be unclogged and was in need of such help. In the morning, the patient is to give himself a coffee enema. He may then discover "gall stone type objects in the stool the following day. These objects are light green to dark green in color, very irregular in shape, gelatinous in texture, and vary in size from grape seeds to cherries."

And now I have good news for you: For those who would like to produce such "gall stone type objects" but prefer to spare themselves the nausea and the coffee enema, I have discovered an alternative to the chiropractor's method. Simply take equal parts of olive oil—any old kind will do—and lemon juice, a small amount of dilute hydrochloric acid (to approximate stomach acid), and mix them well in a cup. Leave this out at room temperature overnight, and voila! You will have the same gelatinous, green, irregularly shaped and sized objects so seductively alluded to in the pamphlet—with a minimum of muss and fuss.

MODERN-DAY QUACKERY

In the last two decades, up-and-coming young quacks have discovered that the American public is obsessed with the stomach. Vitamins, nutrition, and, on the other side of the coin, slimming products, diets, and drugs have all been exploited by snake-oil salesmen. Public appetite for such fare seems limitless, and methods of promotion are many and varied.

Despite scientific evidence that vitamins cure only vitamin-deficiency diseases, there is a large market for megavitamins, mineral supplements, and books advocating megavitamin use. Vitamins advertised as "natural" are identical chemically to "unnatural" vitamins, but cost far more. Like the buyers of Kickapoo Oil, however, many vitamin consumers like to feel that they are getting back to nature when they take vitamin C made from rose hips instead of plain ascorbic acid. Take whichever one you choose; your body won't know the difference.

Self-administered megadosing with vitamins has become

common practice in this country. High dosages of vitamin C are taken to combat the common cold and to increase resistance to disease. Vitamin B6 has enjoyed a recent vogue, and has been taken in excessive amounts for such disparate problems as alcoholism, depression, hypoglycemia, and premenstrual tension. While evidence has accumulated that megadosing with vitamins C and B6 can be harmful, there is no proof that it does any good, except in cases of vitamin-deficiency disease.

The snake-oil doctor is quick to take advantage of health fads. The manufacturers of Laetrile, for example, after nearly twenty years of trying to win FDA approval for the drug, decided to classify the product as vitamin B17. By calling Laetrile a vitamin, they had hoped to avoid the FDA's stringent drug laws. In 1976, however, a federal court in California found that amygdalin, the scientific name for Laetrile, was not a vitamin, and furthermore played no part in human nutrition. In 1977 a federal court in New Jersey found that sale of amygdalin as a food or drug constitutes a fraud on the public.

A deluge of quack publications, overpriced foods, and quack philosophy has resulted from the current popular belief that nutrition can be used to cure practically any ailment. The ways in which this health fad are misused, both by the ignorant and the con artist, are too numerous to mention. As a consumer, you should realize that such diseases as arthritis, heart disease, and cancer are not curable by diet, no matter what the newest book titles and magazine headlines may imply. Most legitimate nutritionists will tell you that white bread is as nutritious as brown bread, and that a diet high in fiber has been proven to be useful in the prevention and alleviation of constipation, but not of cancer.

The quack will make wild and unsubstantiated claims for the superiority of whatever product or theory he is promoting. Usually he will use scare tactics, alternating with promises of miracle cures. Along the same lines, those who tell you that their organically grown vegetables are higher in vitamin content because they have not been grown in chemically depleted soil are wrong. The vitamin content of a vegetable is determined genetically, while its mineral content is absorbed from the soil. Organic vegetables tested for trace pesticides have often contained as much of such chemical material as vegetables that were not organically grown. This is attributed to the fact that soil will retain pesticides for years, and wind and rain can spread pesticides from neighboring fields to an organic farm.

Good nutrition is certainly important, but it is not all the quacks would have you believe. If you want to steer clear of the snake-oil doctor, don't accept everything he tells you on faith. Maintain a little skepticism, and read up on the current scientific literature as it comes out in popular form. Many quacks mouth theories and cite experiments which have been discredited for years, and the public accepts what they say without question.

MAIL-ORDER SEX AND BEAUTY ENHANCERS

Want to be better looking? Improve your sexual powers and increase your pleasure? You bet you do. So does everyone else, and plenty of enterprising scammers are rich today as a result.

A scam with serious, long-term consequences is the promotion of phony "natural" birth control pills. These have been sold door-to-door, through health food stores, and by mail order. In 1977, She-Link Herbal Pill No. 9 was advertised in *Mothering* magazine as a means of preventing conception for six months. All the woman had to do, the instructions said, was take eight pills at one time twice a year, and she would not get pregnant.

Eighty-seven women who took the pills got pregnant

within six months. Two of them were on the *Mothering* magazine staff. The quack behind She-Link, Gee Singh Tong, was found guilty of mail fraud and sentenced to three years in prison.

The desire to be a "manly man" or a femme fatale has not gone out of style and probably never will, no matter what comes out of the closet. Con artists are assured of a market for all kinds of so-called sexual enhancers and vanity products because of widespread insecurity among individuals about their appearance and sexual performance.

In the early 1980s, postal inspectors came across an advertising brochure that aroused their suspicions. Pitching a multivitamin tablet, the brochure made the following claims: "This tested sex pill, NSP-270, is a revolutionary medical discovery for better erections. . . . used in the U.S. Navy penis enlargement and erection improvement program for boys who couldn't measure up to the Navy's standards of manhood . . . who would disgrace the uniform if they ever were allowed to wear it. . . . You can be sure that your erection is getting all the sex nutrient it needs to be 'up to the mark' for maximum sexual performance!"

After investigating the claims made in the brochure, the U.S. Postal Service filed suit against Frank E. Bush, Inc., the promoter of NSP-270, for using the U.S. mails for purposes of fraudulent misrepresentation. Those who think they might benefit from NSP-270 should ask themselves the following questions: Are you a dwarf? If you answered *yes* to the preceding question, is your dwarfism a result of severe zinc deficiency? Those who answered *yes* to both questions might indeed be helped by the active ingredient in NSP-270, or zinc. Otherwise, forget it. The brochure does not mention that the sex nutrient refers to zinc, nor does it give a truthful picture of the study actually conducted by the Navy.

From 1961 to 1963, U.S. Navy Medical Research Unit No. 3 performed an investigation on the role of zinc in human nutrition—*not* an "erection improvement program" as stated in the brochure. The research subjects were not "boys who couldn't measure up to the Navy's standards of manhood," but Egyptian youths whose growth had been stunted by malnutrition, and who were never considered for U.S. military service. The study, moreover, did not conclude that zinc would increase the size of any part of the body except in cases of dwarfism caused by zinc deficiency; then the mineral would promote an overall growth increase. Zinc is plentiful in meats and other animal proteins, and deficiency in this mineral is considered rare in the United States. There was nothing to indicate, in the Navy's study or in any other scientific study, that the addition of zinc supplements to a normal diet improves sexual performance. Overdosing with zinc can be harmful, resulting in abdominal pain, nausea, severe anemia, and fever.

Mark Eden

Your bust will grow right before your eyes ... and grow ... and grow with the new MARK EDEN BUST DEVELOPER. ... You must see a visible improvement on your bust the very first time you use the MARK EDEN and you must add up to three inches or more to your bust the very first week or your money back.
Mark Eden Bust Developer advertisement
Cosmopolitan magazine

Your Slim-Skins are a marvel of ease and simplicity to use. Their ingenious design allows you to convert your own household vacuum cleaner into the most exciting and effective inch reducing machine imaginable. First, get out your vacuum cleaner. Plug it into the electrical outlet nearest to where you plan to do your Slim-Skins program. Now you simply slip on your Slim-Skins over your bare skin, keeping the drawstrings in front. Tie the laces at the waist and knees firmly—but not too tight. The Slim-Skins should always be worn directly over the bare skin; any garment such as pants, slacks, shorts, even light underwear coming between yourself and the Slim-Skins will detract from the real inch trimming potential of this marvelous reducer. After putting on your Slim-Skins, then connect the white universal adapter hose, which is included, by attaching the short nozzled end to the white ring extending from the Slim-Skins. Then attach the longer nozzle on the other end to the hose of your vacuum cleaner. Push the nozzle in until it forms a firm bond. It's just that simple!

Instruction booklet for Slim-Skins

The advertisements quoted above are both for products formerly promoted by Eileen and Jack Feather. The bust developer, sold for close to nineteen years through advertisements in the back of women's magazines and tabloids, was made of two pieces of plastic held together by a spring. By using this contraption as a sort of exercise machine, women were supposed to be able to increase the size of their breasts. (Many readers will doubtless remember the before-and-after photographs featured in these ads. In the "before" shot, the sad-looking model stands, shoulders slumped, in a baggy dress. For the "after" shot, she boasts a cheery smile, a bikini top, and some pretty impressive cleavage.)

Slim-Skins were knickers to which a special adapter hose was provided to use as a hookup with a household vacuum cleaner. According to the promo, the vacuum would perform the weight-reducing work when certain exercises were also performed at the same time.

U.S. Postal Service lawyer Tom Ziebarth, USPS Consumer Protection Division, was involved in litigation with the Feathers for sixteen years, and U.S. attorney Joseph P. Russoniello of the Northern District of California was ready to go to trial charging the Feathers with using the mails to defraud, when the body-beautiful bunco artists finally agreed to settle out of court. Eileen and Jack Feathers paid a nontax-deductible $1.1 million fee to the U.S. Postal Service in exchange for the government's dropping of mail fraud charges. This may sound like a lot of money to fork out, but the Feathers had made a bundle on their bust developers over the years. It is estimated that by 1978 they had grossed about $40 million in Mark Eden sales. They also agreed to stop selling their developer and weight-loss devices until they are able to prove to the FDA that the products are safe and effective for their intended use.

It has been known for many years that there is no way other than pregnancy, lactation, female hormone ingestion, weight gain, or artificial implants to increase breast size. The platform of muscle beneath the breasts can be increased by exercise, but in order for women to add significant muscle bulk, they must take testosterone (male hormone) supplements. The breast itself is made up of fat and glands; its only muscle is in the nipple.

In order to have the bust developer removed from the market, the government needed more specific conclusive evidence that it was ineffective for its intended use. To this end, the Postal Service staged a unique experiment.

Dr. Jack H. Wilmore, former head of the physical education department of the University of Arizona, was selected to perform the research. The subjects who took part in the experiment had responded to an ad in the university paper, the *Arizona Daily Wildcat*. Out of 280 women, seventeen were chosen to be in the experimental group, and seventeen were chosen to make up the control group. First the women's breasts were photographed from front and side views, in both exhalation and full-inhalation position.

Second was the water-displacement test. Women lay in a prone position on a board that allowed the breasts to be suspended in water-filled glass beakers, to be measured by means of water displacement.

Bust measurements were also made by tape measure, both with and without clothing, on the first, second, third, fifth, sixth, twelfth and eighteenth days of the experiment.

The control group did not use the bust developer; the experimental group used it in a daily exercise program for three weeks. No significant change was found in either group; no evidence was found to support claims that the Mark Eden bust developer could increase bust size.

Although the sex nutrients and devices mentioned above have been taken off the market, there are still thousands of bunco remedies and contraptions to choose from, and the marketing methods are much the same. Diet supplements are hot right now; something new will pop up tomorrow, next week, or next month. Don't be fooled if your favorite magazine, which you consider to be reputable, runs full-page ads for rip-offs. And don't believe that because you saw something in print, it must be true. Editors of many otherwise respectable publications think nothing of selling advertising space to people pitching amazing, appetite-satisfying, noncaloric bread; protein powder guaranteed to turn a ninety-pound weakling into the Incredible Hulk; or aphrodisiacs from the enchanted Voodoo Isles. There is no law that says that a publication can be held responsible for the content of these ads, and such ads do help a magazine make ends meet.

QUACKS AND THE LAW

This brings us to the age-old question: Why don't they do something about all these lying, cheating, scheming con artists who advertise their worthless products through the media? And who licenses mail-order advertisers, anyway?

They in this case are the Federal Trade Commission (FTC), the FDA, and the Postal Service. The FTC can prevent dissemination of false and deceptive advertising and unsupported claims for health-care products and drugs. The FDA has the power to administrate many federal laws that require drugs to be properly labeled and contain no harmful ingredients. It also investigates new drugs before they enter the marketplace to ensure that they are safe. The Postal Service can prosecute those who use the mails—in practically any way—to sell their wares deceptively. Mail-order advertisers are not licensed by any governmental agency.

The problem of time is a big one. There are so many cases of fraudulent advertising and false product claims that the organizations authorized to deal with health quackery cannot handle them all. An equally serious problem is the difficulty of proving intent to defraud, even when it is apparent that a remedy, drug, or device does not work for its intended purpose. When the plaintiff is a con artist who specializes in bunco promotions and outrageous sales pitches, he can often convince a jury that his intentions are as pure as the driven snow—or at least leave the jurors guessing. Anyone who can sell hundreds of customers on weekly colonic irrigation has to be a pretty persuasive guy.

REPORTING COMPLAINTS

While laws have been enacted to protect the consumer, many individuals resent such restrictions and insist on seeking out quack health care. And there will always be plenty of con artists ready to answer the call.

If you suspect you have been a victim of quackery, take note of the following:

- False, misleading, or suspect advertising or labeling claims should be reported to the FTC, Bureau of Consumer Protection, Washington, D.C. 20850. Specify

where you saw or heard the ad, and send along a copy
if the ad is in print.

- If the U.S. mail was used to promote or deliver a spur-
ious product, inform your local postmaster, or write to
the Chief Postal Inspector, Washington, D.C. 20260,
sending the advertisement if possible.
- Health frauds can also be reported to your state attorney general's office and county prosecutor's office.

Glossary

Addict. A mark who invests in a scam again and again; a repeater.

Big Con. A big-time confidence game in which the mark is coached to withdraw funds from his account to invest in the scam, i.e., "put on the send."

Big Store. Any establishment "disguised" to resemble a legitimate place of business in order to play a mark. It is carefully furnished to create an impression on the mark and to lull him into a false sense of security.

Bitch. A woman, as in "never pitch a bitch," boiler-room lingo for "never try to do a sales job on a woman." The idea is that a woman is less likely to act on impulse than a man and more likely to consult a spouse, making her more difficult to sway than a man.

Bleat. To complain, especially to the police.

Block Hustle. A scam in which a con man pretends to fence stolen goods for a fraction of their worth. The goods in actuality are cheap, shoddy imitations of expensive merchandise.

Blow-off. A means of getting rid of the mark after fleecing him, without arousing his suspicion.

Boiler Room. A telephone-sales solicitation office; a head-quarters for telephone sales solicitors.

Boodle. A fake bankroll (often comprised of scraps of newspaper) used to deceive the mark. In the short con, it is used to pass for the mark's money. In a big con, it can be made to look like a roll of high-denomination bills when it is actually made up of small bills.

Boost. Shills operating in big-con games.

Broads. Three-card monte; refers to the three queens.

Bumming. *See* slumming.

Bunco. A confidence game (n.); to con (v.); of or pertaining to a confidence game (adj.). From *banca,* a Spanish card game.

Button. A blow-off in which phony police raid a game and the mark is allowed to talk his way out of an arrest.

Cackle Bladder. A way to blow off a mark after he has been fleeced. In a raid or faked attack on one con man by another, a blank is fired. One of the con men has a bladder, or balloon, filled with chicken blood or some reasonable facsimile inside his mouth. He falls, acting as if he had been shot, and allows the blood to trickle from his mouth. Afraid of implication in a murder, the mark flees the scene.

Chill. To lose interest in a con game (for a mark). Also to snub someone, or to stack a deck of cards.

Come Hot. To make a sting whereupon the mark immediately realizes that he has been swindled.

Come-through. A mark who has been fleeced and refuses to be blown off, following the con man in an attempt to get revenge.

Con Mob. The personnel in the big store; the shills, accomplices, and ropers associated with a sting.

Confidence Game. A scam in which theft through guile is practiced, usually in a one-on-one relationship. So called because in order to swindle the mark, the bunco artist must first gain his confidence.

Confidencer. A telephone device that screens out background noise so that only the salesman is audible; used in boiler rooms.

Connection. A dealer, or other source of obtaining illegal drugs, stolen goods, or other contraband.

Convincer. The cash that the con man allows the mark to win in order to *convince* him to speculate for bigger stakes.

Cool a Mark Out. To pacify a fleeced mark.

Cop a Heel. To run away.

Cross Fire. Conversation between two cons, supposedly private, but actually intended to influence an eavesdropping mark.

Double Saw. A twenty-dollar bill.

Drive Call. In phone sales, a high-pressure, follow-up sales pitch delivered over the telephone.

Drop. In phone sales, the "opportunity" offered a tough

customer to purchase half the package, with a so-called free prize thrown in.

Egg. A mark or sucker.

Fall. To be indicted and convicted of a crime.

Fin. A five-dollar bill.

Fix. As in "the fix is in." Cooperation from a bribed policeman. Can also refer to a plan to prevent the mark from going to the police.

Flimflam. Deception; fraud; confidence trick.

Flue. An envelope in which money is placed.

Get a Hard-on. To reach for a gun.

Goat Pasture. Land sold for valueless mineral rights.

Grift. To be on the grift is to be engaged in a racket or criminal profession.

Grifter. A criminal who lives more by his wits than by violence.

Half a C. A fifty-dollar bill.

Heat. Trouble from the police.

Insideman. The member of a con mob who receives marks sent by the roper at the big store.

Kick Back. To give a mark his money back.

Knock a Mark. To convince a mark that he is being swindled. This is notoriously hard to do.

Larceny in the Heart. The inherent tendency to steal or cheat.

Laydown. In phone sales, someone who buys immediately.

Load Call. In phone sales, a repeat call to a recent sucker.

Mack. A romance bunco artist.

Mark. A sucker, or victim.

Mom. An elderly woman who is victimized in a con game.

Monicker. An underworld nickname; for example, "the Yellow Kid."

Mooch. In phone sales, a promising prospect.

Moose Pasture. Selling moose pasture is pitching worthless or nonexistent real estate, mineral rights, mining shares, and so on, usually through a boiler-room operation. The term is Canadian in origin.

Outsideman. Also known as the roper. A con artist who locates a likely mark and brings him into the confidence game.

Payoff. A classic big-con game. The mark is led to believe that he is being allowed to participate in betting on a fixed horse race with guaranteed tips. At first, he plays with money furnished by the cons and is then put on the send for his own money and fleeced.

Payoff Against the Wall. The payoff, without any props, big-store accoutrements, or other setups. The trouble with this game, from the con man's point of view, is that the mark always realizes that he has been swindled.

Play the Chill. To snub. For example, "He played the chill for them."

Poke. A game in which the mark is convinced that he and the outsideman have found a wallet full of money. The mark is told to put up his own money to show his good faith. He eventually gets the wallet, which contains only pieces of newspaper.

Rag. A classic big-con game, similar to the payoff, except that stocks are used instead of races. A mark who is considered to be knowledgeable about stocks is played for the rag, while a mark who knows racing inside and out is played for the payoff.

Rat. A stool pigeon.

Rocks. A con game in which the mark is given some diamonds to have appraised so that he can see that the deal is for real. The diamonds he has appraised are genuine, but those he buys are fake.

Roper. The con man who rounds up and brings in marks to the big store to be fleeced.

Shill. Someone who acts as a decoy for a con artist in order to draw a mark into the con game.

Singer. A person who is paid by the con man to give a glowing reference to marks. He may be in on the scam, or he may actually be given a great deal so that the reference is sincere.

Slumming. A block hustle in which the con claims he is selling stolen merchandise and must immediately leave town and therefore is getting rid of his wares cheap. Also called *bumming.*

Squeal. To tell, inform, rat.

Stall. Keeping a mark on the hook in order to convince prospective marks to bite, and also to gain time before the mark starts to complain.

Sting. The taking of the mark's money in a con game.

Stool Pigeon. Police informer, rat.

Sweetheart Scam. Romance bunco.

Tale. To tell the tale is to give the mark the pitch, explaining how a surefire system works, usually a dishonest one. For example, the con pretends that he has access to the results of a fixed race in advance.

Three Card Monte. A card game. Also called *the broads.*

Widows and Orphans. Unsophisticated and nonwealthy investors who cannot afford to lose out in an investment deal. The term is used derisively by investment salesmen.

Wipe. The mark is convinced to place money in a handkerchief; the handkerchief containing the money is switched, and he ends up with one holding only pieces of newspaper.

Wire. A classic big-con game in which the mark is convinced that he can get in on a system of getting race results in advance of the official announcement by tapping the Western Union wire, or by bribing a W.U. operator to disclose the results a few minutes ahead of the official announcement. The operator then "makes a mistake," and the mark is fleeced and cooled out.

Wise Guys. Mobsters.

Yack. A telephone sales solicitor.

Selected Sources

BOOKS

Abagnale, Frank W., Jr., with Stan Redding. *Catch Me If You Can.* New York: Grosset & Dunlap, Inc., 1980.

Blum, Richard H. *Deceivers and Deceived: Observations on Confidence Men and Their Victims.* Springfield, Ill.: Charles C. Thomas, 1972.

Blundell, Nigel. *The World's Greatest Crooks and Conmen.* London: Books Limited, 1984.

Druggists Circular and Chemical Gazette. Vol. XXX. New York: William O. Allison, 1886.

Ekman, Paul. *Telling Lies.* New York: W. W. Norton & Co., Inc., 1985.

Greene, Robert W. *The Sting Man: Inside Abscam.* New York: E. P. Dutton, 1981.

Health Quackery: Consumer Union's Report on False Health Claims, Worthless Remedies, and Unproved Therapies. New York: Holt, Rinehart, and Winston, Inc., 1980.

Heckstall-Smith, Anthony. *Company of Strangers.* New York: Coward-McCann, Inc., 1960.

Holbrook, Stewart H. *The Golden Age of Quackery.* New York: MacMillan Publishing Co., Inc., 1959.

Hynd, Alan. *The Con Man.* New York: Paperback Library, Inc., 1958.

MacKay, Charles, LL.D. *Extraordinary Popular Delusions and the Madness of Crowds.* Orig. edition, 1841. New York: Noonday Press, 1980.

Maiken, Peter T. *Rip-Off: How to Spot It, How to Avoid It.* Kansas City: Andrews and McMeel, Inc., 1979.

Maurer, David W. *The American Confidence Man.* Springfield, Ill.:
    Charles C. Thomas, 1974.

McClintock, David. *Stealing from the Rich: The Home-Stake Oil
    Swindle.* New York: M. Evans & Co., Inc., 1977.

Melville, Herman. *The Confidence Man: His Masquerade.* Orig. edition,
    1857. New York: W. W. Norton & Co., Inc., 1984.

Parker, Donn B. *Fighting Computer Crime.* New York: Charles Scrib-
    ner's Sons, 1983.

Springer, John L. *Consumer Swindles . . . And How to Avoid Them.*
    Chicago: Henry Regnery Co., 1970.

The Successful Housekeeper: A Manual of Universal Application.
    Detroit: M. W. Ellsworth & Co., 1886.

Suthers, John W., and Shupp, Gary L. *Fraud and Deceit: How to Stop
    Being Ripped Off.* New York: Arco Publishing, Inc., 1982.

Yoors, Jan. *The Gypsies.* New York: Simon & Schuster, Inc., 1967.

ARTICLES

Anderson, Jack. "CIA Role More Than Low Level." *Washington Post,*
    November 2, 1984, p. D-12.

"Behind the Billie Sol Mess." *Newsweek,* May 28, 1962.

"Betty Blair Often Cried During 'Crisis.'" *Denver Post,* December 18,
    1983, p. B-1.

"Bilking Utah's Faithful." *Newsweek,* December 24, 1984.

Braly, David. "How to Spot a Bankruptcy Swindle." *Nation's Busi-
    ness,* October 1983.

"Business Opportunity Swindles." *Consumer's Research,* December
    1984.

Charman, Paul. "Joe Flynn: King of the Sting." *Time Out* (London),
    March 4–10, 1983.

"CIA Complaint to FCC." *New York Times,* December 9, 1984, p.
    E-20.

"CIA Denies a Murder Effort." *New York Times,* September 28,
    1984, p. B-7.

"CIA Told by Judge to Turn Over Data in Ronald Rewald Case."
    Wall Street Journal, March 18, 1985, p. 27.

"CIA vs. ABC: Trying to Punish a Network." *Time,* December 10,
    1984.

"Con Artist Reluctant to Reveal Trade Secrets During CU Speech." *Boulder Daily Camera*, December 6, 1984, p. B-1.

Cornell, James. "Science vs. the Paranormal." *Psychology Today*, March 1984.

"Daring to Be Great." *Newsweek*, August 28, 1978.

"Decline & Fall." *Time*, May 25, 1962.

"Despite Critics and Lawsuits, Herbalife Has Made Mark Hughes Wealthy If Not Healthy." *People*, April 29, 1985.

Eberhardt, Lou. "No More False Hopes from Bust Developer." *FDA Consumer*, October 1983.

"Elderly Get Special Warning on Con Arists." *Denver Post*, June 22, 1983, p. B-1.

"FCC Rejects CIA Complaint." *New York Times*, January 11, 1985, p. A-25.

"FCC Rejects CIA Complaint of News Distortion." *Washington Post*, January 11, 1985, p. A-24.

"The Fine Art of Catching Liars. A Quick How-to Course for Those Who Are Frequently Deceived." *Time*, April 22, 1985.

"Fool's Gold: Downfall of a Bullion Dealer." *Time*, May 9, 1983.

"Franchising: Daring to Be Great." *Newsweek*, September 11, 1972.

Freifeld, Karen, and Engelmayer, Sheldon. "Male Fraud." *Health*, November 1983.

"Funds Seized in 'Boiler Room' Probe." *Denver Post*, March 18, 1984, p. D-1.

Harris, Marlys. "America's Capital of Fraud." *Money*, November 1983.

———. "The Man Who Gulled Hawaii." *Money*, December 1983.

Hawkins, Nance. "The Williamson Gang Still Rides." *National Centurion*, September 1983.

Hilton, John. "Doing the Motown Hustle." *Car and Driver*, July 1983.

Hiltzik, Michael A. "Your Money—Buying Gold and Silver." *50 Plus*, February 1984.

Hynd, Noel. "The Gold-Plated Con: A Scam that Didn't Pan Out." *50 Plus*, February 1984.

"Imposter Suspect Jailed." *Denver Post*, November 17, 1983, p. B-5.

Kraar, Louis. "How George Tan Duped His Bankers." *Fortune*, November 14, 1983.

Lidz, Frank. "The Game of the Name: Bunco Artist Arthur Lee Trotter Likes to Pose as Sports Star in His Scams." *Sports Illustrated*, September 19, 1983.

"Low Profile in Texas." *Newsweek*, November 3, 1975.

Lowther, William. "Star-crossed Lovers." *Maclean's*, April 7, 1980.

"The Man and the Martians." *Newsweek*, February 21, 1972.

Moine, David J. "To Trust, Perchance to Buy." *Psychology Today*, August 1982.

Morganthau, Tom, and Collier, Randy. "The Man with 105 Wives." *Newsweek*, February 21, 1983.

Neuhaus, Cable. "Scorned and Swindled by Her Bigamist Husband, Sharon Vigliotto Got Mad, Then Got Even." *People*, April 12, 1982.

Nicholson, Tom, and Sigale, Merwin. "A Pyramid Crumbles in Miami." *Newsweek*, July 13, 1981.

"The Other Cheek." *Newsweek*, February 4, 1963.

"Phone, Postal Rip-Offs Show Increase Here." *Denver Post.* April 3, 1983, p. B-1.

"Phone-Sale Losses Put in Millions." *Denver Post.* June 17, 1983, p. A-20.

"Postal Fraud Caseload Climbing." *Denver Post,* April 3, 1983, p. B-1.

"Promoters: Fast Buck Gospel." *Time*, November 29, 1971.

"Reach Out and Bilk Someone." *Time*, October 24, 1983.

"A Scandal Hot as a Pistol." *Life*, July 1, 1962.

Schroeder, Jay. "Gypsy Crime in America. *National Centurion*, September 1983.

Stern, Richard L. "Now You See It, Now You Don't." *Forbes*, June 20, 1983.

"The 'Stock-Fraud Capital' Tries to Clean Up Its Act." *Business Week*, February 6, 1984.

"Turning Up the Heat on the 'Boiler-Room' Scams." *Business Week*, November 14, 1983.

"Verdict in Texas." *Time*, April 5, 1963.

"A Visit with Billie Sol Estes." *Newsweek*, October 12, 1964.

"We Stole . . ." *Newsweek*, April 8, 1963.

"Winning by Losing." *Newsweek*, April 8, 1963.

Index